intimate notebooks of the philosopher at work, revealing his processes of thought as he questions theories and seeks answers to the eternal questions which men have asked since the beginning of civilization.

In this wise and thoughtful book, *The Making of Men*, Professor Weiss turns his philosophical thinking to education and offers practical suggestions well within the parents', educators', and administrators' means to encompass. From his long experience as an educator he discusses subjects ranging from art to zoology and when, where, and how they should be taught to be of the greatest value to the potentially fulfilled man. He discusses the role of the teacher in elementary and secondary schools and compares the educational systems in the universities of Continental Europe, Great Britain, and the United States.

The last three chapters of this provocative book deal with mature men: the kind of lives most men lead once their formal education has been completed and the kind of lives they could and should lead in the business and social world if in their formative years they had been prepared for more than just a job or career. Despite large-scale educational opportunities for both the youth and the adult and despite the shortened workweek and workday which leaves most men ample leisure time to spend on their particular interests, men are still woefully far from being fulfilled. But this state of being need not continue if those responsible for the making of men will envision a man as an ideally complete being, which, in the tradition of Plato, Aristotle, and, in more recent times, Hegel, Professor Weiss makes abundantly clear for all to see.

PAUL WEISS is Sterling Professor of Philosophy at Yale University. A Harvard Ph.D., where he studied under Alfred North Whitehead, he taught at Harvard, Radcliffe, and Bryn Mawr before going to Yale in 1945 as a Visiting Professor. A year later he was made a full Professor and in 1962 given the Sterling chair appointment. He lectures widely, both here and abroad, and is among the leading educators whose opinions are most often sought on matters of national interest. His book *Modes of Being* was the only current philosophical work selected for inclusion in the White House library during President Kennedy's administration.

THE MAKING OF MEN

THE MAKING OF MEN

Paul Weiss

Southern Illinois University Press, Carbondale and Edwardsville

Feffer & Simons, Inc., London and Amsterdam

Copyright © 1967, by Southern Illinois University Press
Library of Congress Catalog Card No. 67–10046
Printed in the United States of America
Designed by Andor Braun

For Charles Hartshorne,
Philosopher and Friend

Preface

I HAVE TAUGHT for some thirty-five years. But I am not sure when I have been most successful or effective, and when I have failed to achieve even a minimal desirable result. Neither student nor colleague, with rare exceptions, does much to help the teacher know himself as he is known. I cannot, then, with any confidence draw upon my own experiences or the experiences of others for knowledge, guidance, or principles relevant to educational theory. But over the course of this same period I have reflected a good deal about the nature of reality and the fundamental concepts which govern knowledge and action. I have given considerable thought to the foundations of ethics and the proper end of man. It is to these I have looked to help me find my way through that pervasive and yet almost ungraspable process we call education.

I have rewritten the entire book a number of times, in part to meet the penetrating criticisms of Vernon Sternberg, publisher and friend, and of Richard Sewall, colleague and friend. I am not entirely satisfied with it yet, but I think there is little that I now can do to improve it.

P. W.

New Haven, Conn.
January, 1966

Contents

		Page
	Preface	*vii*
1	The Life of the Child	3
2	The Tween-Age	31
3	On the Verge of Manhood	63
4	The College Curriculum	77
5	The Lives Men Lead	111
6	Leisure Time	128
7	The Good Life	141
	Index	153

THE MAKING OF MEN

I

The Life of the Child

A CHILD IS A CHILD. Nothing could be more obvious. Yet nothing has been so misunderstood.

A child is a child. It is not a noisy savage, noisy and savage though it be. It is not an angel, pure and innocent. Nor is it a leaky animal, though it does leak. A child is a child.

We are not really attending to the child when we say that it is an incipient man or a prospective citizen. We surely abuse it when we spend all our energies preparing it for work, for college, or even for citizenship. More often than not, the better our preparation, the greater our abuse.

Teach it we should. Teach it we must. Teach it we do. But we should not teach it what we want it to learn. The child should be taught only what it should learn. And what is this? To be a child. Nothing more? Nothing more.

Is this not to turn the child loose to learn whatever its whim and impulse dictate? Left to itself it is unfocused; denied guidance it loses direction. If not trained and disciplined, the child will interfere with us and harm itself. A child is a child, but it must be helped if it is to become fully a child. We must give it opportunities to exercise its childish powers. It must be taught.

What shall we teach the child? To begin with, nothing. Teach the child something too early, and it is given at once too little and too much; the size of its world is unnecessarily reduced and its content overspecified. All that is important for the child to know, it already confronts in a confused, rather chaotic form. What it must learn is to share more in a world of which it is already a part. We do it a disservice when we force it too soon to devote its energies to the mastery of some arbitrarily selected segment of the world.

2]

A child has a past. Once it had been an infant, dependent and helpless. Nor was it easy for it or for others to move it to the stage where it could feed itself, control its bladder and its bowels, talk and listen, walk and rest, be joyous and yet obedient. Forever it bears the marks of the slow process by which it reached the place where it is a functioning child.

In its short life the child learned a good part of a very difficult lesson: it learned how to get along with its parents and siblings. Like the infant, the child is a familial being, living, not in society at large, but in a part of it, half-sealed off from the rest. Were the child placed outside the family it would be almost as helpless as the infant, unable to sustain or to protect itself.

Parents and siblings soon channelize the infant's initial random and ineffective acts. They teach it to have a distinctive place, and to act with some awareness of the presence and rights of others. Rarely is the infant given specific instructions; example, backed by suggestion and criticism, are the primary means by which it is taught. Explanations are rarely offered to it, nor are they often wanted. Those who mold the infant normally know little of the reasons behind what they demand of it, but that does not prevent them from gradually altering its rhythms and emphasizing its responsibilities until it fits within a rather stable and powerful pattern.

Both the infant and the child are forced to conform,

made to obey, kept in line. And there is wisdom in this. Both must be kept inside the family for their own good, until they are strong enough in body and mind to make at least a partial escape.

At its best, the family is a web of injustice and misunderstanding; nowhere else is there so much bitterness, willfulness, and folly. But even when it has strayed far from an ideal course, the normal family continues to be quickened by the enriching love that the parent has for the child. It is not a wise love. At once too selfish and too selfless, it is often oversolicitous and usually quite unimaginative. Parental love is almost always tinged with fear and worry. Rarely can it avoid giving ground before the insistent demands of other members of the family and of society, though again and again it breaks through these and other constraints to allow the parent to make direct contact with the child.

A child properly loved, trusts, accepts itself. It becomes aware of its worth. It imitates and participates. Engaging in common tasks and speech, it comes to share in a common familial outlook to which it contributes more and more as time goes on. But most important, the love annihilates itself. Gradually it moves the child to the point where familial love is not wanted. If the child is fortunate this is also the point at which the love is no longer given, at least in its familiar form. In its place the child will find affection and concern—and, hopefully, some understanding.

3]

The traumatic experience of birth is followed by a woeful weaning. After being pushed into a world of surprises, some of which frustrate or frighten, the infant finds that its appetites and desires are defied again and again. It then learns the bitter lesson that love is episodic, that it fluctuates, and that it has many objects. The infant soon learns the sad truth that its mother is not always at the center of the world.

No family is altogether cut off from the larger world beyond. Nor is there a clean boundary separating family from school. While in the family, the infant and the child in work and in play make some contact with the outside world. But it was in the course of familial life that they learned that their mother's love had limits, and that her patience can come to an end.

No mother ever loved an infant or a child exactly as it needed to be loved. Everyone loves too much and too little, at the wrong times and in the wrong ways. All of us are oversolicitous; all underattentive. No one has a rhythm which exactly matches that of another. But what love fails to achieve in detail, it makes up in depth. The mother's love can be relied upon for the most part; it can be readily elicited. Against it as a background the members of the family live at their best. Even when they inevitably and often gladly attend to other ways of being taught and supported, the love that bound them is not altogether lost.

4]

It has taken the teachings and the pleadings of a galaxy of geniuses to persuade some of the world that a child is a child. Rousseau, Pestalozzi, Froebel, and Montessori made this their central theme. They also urged that children be loved by the teacher. This was an inevitable conclusion for them, since they dealt with children who had been deprived of a good life in a family. These thinkers offered substitutes for the family situation, and this meant that they had to see that the love, which had been denied a place in a family or had been severely curtailed there, was provided by others.

Only rarely can a teacher love a child. And when she does, she usually does what she should not do. She then tends to smother the child in affection, thereby taking from it the need to forge a place for itself in a world of children, surrounded by a world of adults.

What the child needs from the teacher is not love, but sympathy. Like love, sympathy exhibits a primary concern for the good of another. It too is alert to the fact that the child needs satisfaction now. Like love, sympathy is also ready to forgive. It too is willing to overlook faults; it too is quickened by a desire to accept the individual for what he is, and to bring out the richness that is latent. But sympathy is a little more sensitive than love is to the need to discipline the child and to instill good habits in it. And unlike love sympathy does not involve a self-exposure.

To love is to open oneself up to a misunderstanding, to endless demands and perhaps to a rebuff. It is to stand naked, with one's defenses down. Even the infant can sense this. It is a tyrant, with its mother as subject. With some relief she therefore sees it turn into a child. But it will do this well only if it is weaned from the world of love. In moving from home to school, from family to classroom and playground, the child should lose the support that love provides. In its place, if fortunate, the child will meet with a sympathetic understanding that will enable it to deal with new topics in new ways.

There is no one moment when the infant ceases to be an infant and emerges as a child. There is no one moment when the child vanishes only to be replaced by the youth. The passage from one stage to the other is hardly perceptible. The pace of one individual is different from that of another, precluding the use of calendars and calipers as proper measures of growth. This does not mean that there are no powers or features which allow one to speak with accuracy of the life and world of the infant in contrast with that of the child or the youth, or of these in contrast with the life and world of the young man and the mature human being. But it does mean that we should attend to the fact that while some mature rapidly others mature slowly, that chronological age is but a number and not a statement of the nature of the body or the mind, or of their capacity to act or grow.

The sudden increase in population, combined with a confidence in the value of education, however, has produced a pressure to favor the one who matures rapidly. We have allowed him to become a part of a new world before he has in fact departed from another. Not yet having accomplished anything he is in danger of accomplishing nothing later. We would be kinder if, instead of speaking of him as successful, we thought of him as a problem.

Living is a ripening; the child must be allowed to mature. Even when its mind is quick and its skills exceptional, it has only the mind and the skills of a child. They are embryonic, not developed, functioning more or less uncontrolled, without clear goal or affiliations.

5]

A child deserves a future. It will get it only if we allow it a present. This it has already partly won for itself. To deny it its present is to deny it some of its rights, its achievements, and its promise.

It is only when the child has lived outside the family in the school or playground that it first becomes a child, ready to be taught to be a child to the full. Of course no school ever replaces the family; the school should be content to do no more than supplement and continue the family's work. If the school does less, it will provide little more than an interlude between the periods when the family is in control. But it is also true that if it tries to be more than a supplement, it will be unjust to both family and child; excessive schooling keeps from the child some of the love it needs and deserves to have.

The child lives in a world of its own. It has its own time scale, its own spatial distances. Causality has a different meaning for it than for adults. The child's attention span is long enough for the expression of its characteristic curiosity and for its self-exploration and experimentation, but rarely long enough to enable the child to engage in any significant task. We hurt it when we squeeze it into a seat unsuited for its feet, its back, and its hands; we cheat it when we force it to repeat by rote what interests neither it nor us; and we distort it when we make it live as though it were just an adult but of small size.

No one wants a child to run a family or a business; it is neither wise enough nor mature enough to do justice to them or to itself. For the very same reason, no one should want it to act or to speak like an adult. It cannot and ought not to be forced to think or work in any other than child-like ways. Most important, it must be allowed to play only as children can. Sometimes a child tries to live up to the ideals it supposes adults would like it to attain. It becomes too good to be a good child. I devoted my only sonnet to that theme.

THE GOOD CHILD

Forever wanting less, needing more, shyly passionate,
Fearing to love, fearing hate, self overthrown,
Too soon you take the shape of man full-grown,
Poor, stunted, self-effacing marionette.
So reasonable, far outside good reason's net,
Lured by obedience's quieting to a life alone,
You offer virtue a body lacking bone,
And confine it there with an endless etiquette.
Good child, make yourself, for goodness' sake, be bad,
Let what is conquer the childish should,
Make self with self-respect once more be glad,
Come try again to live in a world that's rude,
Give up this hope to will good will. It's mad.
With good reason, dear child, be not so good.

An infant plays a little; the child plays a good deal of the time. That play is not an anticipatory form of work; a child knows too little to have such anticipations. Nor is the child ready to share in complicated games—play structured by rules to which all submit. Even the most mature child is unprepared to benefit from such discipline. And of course it is unable to engage in sports. In a sport a grown body is tested against other bodies and the relentless passage of time, the limits of space, and the law-abiding course of nature, in the effort to discover what a man has mastered, what he can endure, and how dextrous and spontaneous he can be while keeping to the rules. The child has far to go before it can move from play to games, to sport, and to work.

Puppies and kittens may play in anticipation of a full participation in serious living. But we have no warrant for supposing that the child blindly, like a puppy, prepares himself to become an adult. Neither the child nor the adult is in a natural state. The world they inhabit is artifactual, governed mainly, not by drives or biological urges, but by tradition, habits, and discipline.

In play the child uses and helps make the world in which it lives. Throughout Spain it plays at bull fighting; all over the United States it plays with balls. The different environments are reflected in the different forms of play but not duplicated there. Instead, a new world is created in which only children are a part.

The child makes an artificial world, something no puppy can do. That world is produced through play, an achievement not possible to an adult. Because the child is human it plays as no animal will, to produce what no animal can envisage. Because it is a child, it plays as no adult can, to make what no adult wants.

A humanlike doll is not needed by a child who wishes to play at being a doctor or a mother. A simple stick will do as well as any doll with human hair and eyes that open and close. The child needs no uniform to enable it to act the part of a nurse or a policeman. To express authority the child thrusts out its lip and speaks sternly; a uniform does not increase its sense of power.

A child quickly tires of its toys. Why not? They are little more than the expression of the failure of adults to imagine what a child is and needs. A stick is a baby for a child; so is a doll. But adults think that only a doll will really serve. Yet the doll is no more of a baby than a stick is. Both are inanimate; both must be enlivened by the child's imagination.

Unless perverse and perverted, a child does not play for adults any more than it plays to be an adult. It does not even play for other children. It plays with them. With them it forges a world in which they can live, a world that is momentarily articulated, now in this way and now in that, for no other purpose than that of allowing the child to be together with other children. A child lives in a world of children. That world is surrounded by men and things which it takes for granted because and so far as it has been granted a life of its own.

Our courts are slowly beginning to see that a child has rights, over against the society, over against its parents, over against whatever else there be. The recognition is slow and halting, but daily it becomes more and more widespread. Psychiatrists and social workers have also come—and brought the rest of us—a long way toward recognizing the distinctive problems and solutions which are pertinent to the child. The child has rights which deserve protection—particularly the child's right to play as a child.

The child is being educated when it plays; its play is its medium of instruction. To teach it best we must allow it to play. Given opportunities to express itself in multiple ways, it will find a place for itself in a world of children, a world that play creates. Forced from play, riveted in a seat before an adult who is ready to rigidify the child's mind as well as its body, it will play in defiance, and play when it can, but never as well as it should.

The child, like everyone else, can be satisfied and fulfilled only in the present. Either we deny it fulfillment then, in the hope that it will be fulfilled in some presumably superior way in the future—where we hope it will arrive—or we allow it to be as complete now as a child can possibly be. If the former be our choice, it may well turn out that the child is never satisfied, never completed. We will have made it deal solely with means which might never get it to a desired end. Only if we attend to the fulfillment of the child now, can we do justice to its rights to be a person. Because it is a human being exercising human powers it must be permitted to express itself, to find some modicum of happiness in its world. It has the right to become and live as a full child.

6]

In its early stages childish learning is indistinguishable from childish play. Like it, it is random and somewhat free. Both are multifaceted, at once serious and joyous, with concentration and inattention flowing quickly into one another. The child learns while it plays, and plays with what it learns. This is how it spends much of its time before it goes to school; this is how it should spend its time while in school. The wise teacher will allow the child in school to continue to play while it learns; the child will then not be so anxious to escape from the classroom to the street, the yard, and the home. Unfortunately, the school day too often serves as little more than a forced stop in the process of true learning.

The best beginning is made by a teacher who acts as a sympathetic older companion, ready to provide the child with appropriate opportunities. She helps the child to share in a traditional outlook, to sharpen its discriminations, to exercise its rights correctly, and to respect the rights of others. No one has found a better way of achieving all these desirable results than through the telling of a story— almost any story.

A child's story need not have well-defined characters

or plot; it need not be inspiring or informative. Later, good, well-organized, and well-written stories can replace the almost pointless, plotless tales that so delight and teach the young. There will then be time enough to supplement storytelling with formal instruction in special areas and topics. But if the earlier stage be skipped or slighted in the anxious effort to begin formal instruction, something of the dash of the child's world will be slowed, some of its color will be grayed, and the child's sense of wonder will be dulled where not denied.

Daily existence, for the adult as well as for the child, is overrun with confusions, irregularities, and irrelevancies. Its consistency and order are only precariously maintained against a perpetual and ever-chancing intrusion by strong powers. To sense what existence is in essence one needs the guidance of art. The fortunate child is one allowed to learn about existence through the art of the story. It then learns everything and nothing—the nature of the whole but filled out with fantasy rather than with fact.

"Once upon a time," the child's story begins. When is that? The child knows. It is not some day in the past with a date to be arrived at by subtracting from a number attached to the present. It is "any time," "all the time," when nothing ever happened, but which is at the base of all that happens. "Once upon a time" is when and where wild animals can be together with civilized men, where golden virtue defeats ugly vice, where innocence struggles successfully with burning malice, and folly is exposed to the laughter of all. It is a value-laden world, where all is either good or evil, right or wrong.

The story brings child and teacher to the heart of the mystery of existence. It at once exposes the mystery and adds to it. From the story the child readily learns something of the careers open to hope and fear; it there gets to know the weights and the rewards of bravery, industry, and patience. It is a singular child indeed who neglects these to attend instead to fairies, princes, chimney sweeps, magic swords, birds, and wolves in old women's night clothes. These serve merely to carry the story and what it is to convey. They are not beings to be remembered, imitated, or reflected upon, though large industries are built on the notion that this is what attracts the child and perhaps educates it.

A story is not a report. It offers no set of facts, no empirical truths, no advice. When a moral is drawn, when the story is made to sustain preaching, formal lessons and the like, the child loses interest. Compelled to listen, the child will live through the lessons as part of the price it must pay in order to enjoy the story.

The child settles down to hear the story. Ready to pass out of its daily world into another, its first act is one of reorientation. It begins by accepting the storyteller and incidentally, therefore, the author, the characters, and the incidents as part of a world it faintly knows. The storyteller is at home in the world of the story, and the child, to enjoy and learn from the story, accepts the storyteller and his tale. It trusts the storyteller; it relies on him to make evident that innocence and virtue in the listener, in the story, and in fact will be forever protected and justified.

The child gives itself to the story. More quickly and surely than the adult, it lives in and with the story, and thereby comes to grasp something of the texture and the lilt of the world from which it had momentarily turned away. It identifies itself in the story with the young, the innocent, and the good as environed by brute and thoughtless force. The story thereby serves as an epitomization of the entire scheme of things, which must be mastered if the child is to be able to maintain itself against brute reality, which is to say, if it is to freely be.

The story teaches in a double way. By identifying itself with the virtuous, triumphant dimensions of the story, the child becomes alert to existence as at once dynamic, open-ended, and ordered. It then discerns something of the steady aspect of existence, an aspect which had been obscured by the fleeting particularities of daily life. Without reaching express formulation, the child then comes to know that there are final realities to which it can turn in success and in misfortune. This lesson is learned at no particular time and in no particular way. Awareness of finalities is achieved mainly through a telling and a retelling of stories. The child though never comes to the point where it has these finalities in clear focus. But also it never loses all hold on them and what they import for it. Long ago the adult learned that the light in which he now stands fades off imperceptibly into a final darkness. As a child he was alert to that darkness in a way he rarely is today, as at once ominous and inviting, wondrous and dismaying.

The story turns the child toward the horizon of experience, but it would dislocate the child did it not at the same time enable the child to find a place in its own world. In submitting to the presence of the finalities which it discerns, the child at the same time accommodates itself to the presence of other beings, and particularly of other children. It comes to know something of their needs and desires; it senses their resistance and learns the strength of their appetites; at its best it is aware of their rights. Gradually the child will come to see itself as one among other children, all trembling, ignorant centers of hope and fear.

A child's story is simple in structure; it has little or no plot. Rarely is the movement of the story steady or smooth. Instead, episode crowds hard on episode; sudden threat and disaster are followed quickly by sudden relief and reward. Each character seems to be subsumable under a single adjective. No occurrence seems to need supports or reasons; each takes place without apparent cause or neighbors. Despite that, a child's story is a kind of truncated myth, since it combines an insight into final realities with a belief that the course of the world is under good and strong control. The incidents, and incidentally the characters of the story, convey to the child not only something of the eternal and right, but also something of the way in which all beings impinge on one another. It learns through them how all are affected by what had been and which now, in the story, is had again. As a consequence the child alters its expectations and modifies its attitudes toward itself and others.

7]

The child needs to be formally educated, taught specific things. It must master the techniques of reading and writing; it must learn how to think better; it must improve its discrimination and its methods of exploration. The child must be formally taught about the past it shares with others, the present in which it now lives, and the future it will someday occupy and perhaps partly possess. Without such knowledge it would be but dimly aware of itself, and of the things with which it must, sooner or later, interplay. Such knowledge need not, such knowledge should not depart from the area opened up in the story. The truths of the story are articulated in formal education, and thereby enabled to be firmly and explicitly possessed. Formal instruction for the child is storytelling, fractionated into a number of specialized activities, pursued with rigor.

There would be no need to follow up the telling of a story with formal instruction were the child forever to remain a child, or could it automatically slip, with a change in date, into the posture of a youth. But this never happens. As the child grows older it also grows. It gets bigger, becomes more adroit; it becomes stronger and better able to insist on itself. New urges, stronger impulses, larger needs irresistibly crowd to the fore. The child probes; it questions; it is curious and flexible. None of this though makes it probable that the child will become a full-fledged child or a normal youth. To arrive at these positions it must be taught, formally taught. And there is no better place to teach it than in school.

Education is an art. Its tools are teachers and books; its media words and acts. Its primary task is to reconstitute the young so that good can be maximally achieved in and by them, leading them to move on until they reach the point where they are enlightened, freed men. The art is practiced both inside and outside the school. Educational institutions are in fact primarily laboratories where the art can be pursued under ideal conditions and expert guidance. They are not indispensable. Men have succeeded in becoming very well educated outside the confines of educational institutions. But these were exceptional men. The vast majority needs the help of teachers. From the beginning almost everyone needs guidance in reading; almost everyone needs a teacher to introduce him to the subtler delights of learning and knowing. And that teacher teaches best who stands before his students as a mature and cultivated man, sympathetically alert to the promise and limitations of the young.

In this country we have developed a hierarchy of institutions which concern themselves with different stages and phases of education. Their order roughly answers to the age groups of students. In addition, we have forged a number of combinations of institutions, new to history, of which the American university is one signal product. In both the hierarchy and the synthesis of institutions there is and should be some overlapping, because neither men nor their interests fit neatly into any compartments, and because continuity and interplay are promoted by having students and interests impinge on one another in multiple ways.

The hierarchy has at least four members: the primary school, the secondary school, the college, and the professional and graduate schools. The first, of course, is the school for the child. Ideally it enables the child to conform effectively to some of the prevailing customs of act and thought. Unfortunately this too often has meant that the schools have spent their energies teaching children how to belong to a society which had largely vanished by the time the children were qualified to be functioning parts of it. In fear of this folly, primary schools in recent years have been so anxious to make children fit into the world which is yet to be, that they have neglected to attend sufficiently to the need to communicate something of the wisdom and knowledge that had been achieved over the centuries. Such errors can be avoided if the decision as to what is to be taught is grounded in an acknowledgment of an ideal good. We must know what kind of world children ought to live in now and later; it alone justifies our including in the curriculum not only reading, writing, and arithmetic, but art appreciation and the study of nature.

The items which the child is to master are simple. The outlook which is to be communicated to it is broad and general. To avoid looseness and incoherence the whole must be sustained by an insistence on some exactitude. Exactitude must not, however, be equated with punishment; it has its own value and its own delights. To teach the child to be exact is to enrich, not to curb it. Learning can be enjoyable even when subject to restraints and hard demands, provided only that those who teach understand that disciplining is not an end in itself, and that what is taught is to serve as a ground and basis for what is to be encountered later.

What is taught in the schools, and the discipline which is integral to that teaching, is in a different way also taught in the home, church, and playground. The work of the school receives a needed supplement in those places. In the last analysis, the elementary school teacher is at the same time almost a parent, a religious leader, and a coach, and they, in turn, are hard to distinguish or separate from her.

The elementary school offers an idealized situation, where distractions are minimal and concern is directed toward enabling the child to be fulfilled, and thereby to be eventually enabled to attend and respond to invitations to live as a youth. In the ideal school the learning process is focused on under the best conditions. There one can concentrate on the task of education, freed from incursions of the workaday world. But the ideal school is nowhere to be found. Instead of being a place where a child is gladly taught and where it gladly learns, the school in fact has often become a place where the child resentfully builds up a refusal to be educated further by teachers who do not care to educate it at all. The fault is hardly the child's. It has been taught badly. We can avoid the bad teaching by leaving the child alone. But then, as has already been observed, we leave it to its own devices and vagaries. The proper alternative to bad teaching is not no teaching, but good teaching. Only good teaching satisfies the child's needs and respects its rights, and in that act turns the child into a youth ready to be taught new things and in another way.

The child has a ten year life, from two to twelve or so. It needs and ought to be formally educated. It ought to know and to master the instruments and agencies by which further growth could be achieved and further knowledge acquired. It is the awareness of this truth that helped sustain those who insisted that the child be subject to rote-learning. To learn by rote, to memorize the meaningless, the atomized, the detached, and the fragmentary is to learn to submit; it is to become habituated and perhaps obedient and disciplined. Rote-learning enables the child to make use of tools without reflection, thereby freeing its mind for more important tasks. Insistence on rote-learning can therefore be justified—were it not for another truth that the advocates of rote-learning overlook. Rote-learning encourages lassitude or passivity, where it does not arouse rebellion. In almost every case it slackens the interest, for it is confessedly a method for making the child focus on what is uninteresting both in itself and to the child. The child has an active mind. This should be structured by the teacher, not subdued or turned into a storehouse of disconnected facts.

It is a mistake to cater to the child. It does not know what it wants or what is good for it; it does not know what could be given to it. To see the child as a child does not mean that it is to be left childish, an unformed creature which lives through experiences, but neither investigates nor matures. It must be given work that is appropriate to its powers and its possible satisfactions. Sometimes it must be made to think and to act, to attend and to work in direct opposition to its express desires. But that does not preclude giving it interesting material; it should not preclude its being taught by someone interested in it.

The child should be taught to read. Only through reading can it learn to exercise its imagination and yet come to know what is beyond its experience and vision. Ideally, it is to be taught to read the stories it likes to hear, but that stage can be reached only after it has spent considerable time learning how to read.

Practicing how to read is not identical with mastering a vocabulary. Vocabulary offers stones; what is wanted is a building. From the very beginning the child must read as well as listen to stories, not to words or sentences. The point will be missed if it be supposed that reading is a process of sounding words one after the other on the basis of cues before the eyes.

Reading is the art of following the rationale of a subject—which is more than simply understanding what a sentence or a paragraph means. What is read has a structure and introduces one to the structures characteristic of men and other realities. The good reader has a different pace and rhythm at different times, sensitive to the fact that words and sentences have different colors and weights in different places. Here this or that word or sentence must be emphasized or savored; in another place the same word or sentence must be muted, rushed through, or hardly noticed. That to which the words refer has boundaries, consequences, opponents and kinsmen; one reads well only if he is aware of these.

He who reads a newspaper and a poem in the same way, reads one, and perhaps both improperly. The point is overlooked—indeed it is in fact directly denied by those who urge all to speed up their reading. Nothing is said about what should be done with the saved time, perhaps because it is assumed that this time is well-accounted for. But then slow reading is thought to cut into time that could have been more profitably spent elsewhere. But the good use of spare time is a skill few have mastered. If it is to be wasted, why not waste it in slow reading?

Each person should read as well and as fast as he can, but according to the demands of the subject matter and the style in which it is presented. In some cases what needs to be taught is how to read slower than is usually the practice. Science, poetry, and geometry are best read when read in slow time. Since almost everyone has been brought up on material which deserves to be read only rapidly, he who would master other material must be trained to change his pace from normal to slow.

A shift in pace can take place well or badly, at the right or at the wrong time. We can teach the way to do it at the start by reading in accordance with the different demands made by distinctive styles and the various parts of the story, and by formal teaching of what had already been presented in a story. Good reading will never be the accomplishment of one who allows only his eyes to move; both the mind and the imagination must be employed. And that takes effort on the part of both the teacher and the student. The result should be an awareness of the texture of language and the shape of what it is to convey.

Good reading is subject to a double condition: it is governed by the author, and it attends to the logic of the subject matter. Writing is more demanding and more self-centered, since it is primarily an originative, creative art. Not primarily a form of self-expression or an agency of communication, it offers a public, effective way for making articulate what otherwise would remain blurred or unnoticed. It has many functions. It can serve as a source of communication, as a medium of expression, or as an opportunity to elaborate, but only if it is not confused with the art of calligraphy, or the technique of using pen or typewriter. Writing too must attend to the logic of the subject matter, changing its course to keep in accord with changes in topic and situation.

The basic training of the child should be given and controlled by its speech, broken up for convenience's sake into reading and writing. Reading and writing are in fact initially sedimentations and solidifications of speech itself, and in all reading and writing there is an incidental use of speech. They have distinctive rationales and rights, but these are all acquired later, when they have been marked out as distinctive enterprises, doing distinctive things.

In speech the creative and spectator sides of language are fused and enhanced; it is by speech that a person is exteriorized. Through it he makes evident the nature of his person and the way he fits in the world. His speech reveals the control he has of his language, and through this the control he has over his thoughts and the world outside them. Yet despite the great importance of speech, most educators do not overly occupy themselves with understanding its nature and demands, and the way in which its best use can be promoted. They neglect it in part because they exaggerate the value of learning a language informally. Most of our speaking, to be sure, is learned in this way in the course of daily living. And what is so learned is unduplicable. Informal learning enables us to be at ease with the language, to readily absorb its characteristic idioms, and to be ready to use its more important turns and powers. But informal learning also encourages the slurring of important distinctions and keeps the mind at the level of unreflective judgment.

The language of everyday is a language of pragmatic classifications and distinctions appropriate only for the rough commerce of social living. To attend only to everyday language is to reduce the need and temptation to use language with freshness and effectiveness, with full sensitivity to its manifold possibilities. Language should be formally as well as informally taught.

There are places where children are cozened into the practice of speaking publicly in imitation of debaters or of lawyers and preachers—themselves supposed to be something like debaters. This would be a wise practice were the main object of discourse the persuading and conversion of others, and were the child an apprentice who had to learn the best tactics for changing the minds of others. But speech is at its most vital in conversation, and is at its best when it serves to forge a communion with others.

The child's need and use of speech are different from those of older human beings. Children are no more ready to converse or to be in communion with others than they are to read or write, to listen to stories, to add sums, or to study geography when these are geared to adult mentality and attention spans; but they are ready if these activities are properly scaled for them.

Children have conversational patterns and needs which are different from those characteristic of the more mature. Those patterns and the way they are to be embodied, those needs and the way they are to be satisfied, can be discovered and supported only by teachers who sympathetically encourage children to speak as children, in a world of children, set inside a human world, itself environed by nature. The children of course are to be taught not to lisp or to mumble, even if this be the way most children speak. Treating them as children does not mean that they should be allowed to be childish.

Speaking well can be an art. Like all art, it should be taught by those who have mastered it, and who are appreciative of the fact that others are to master it also, but in distinctive, individual ways. And what is true of speaking is true of the other arts taught to the child.

Arithmetic has always been part of the elementary

curriculum. The reason has rarely been made clear. We can justify its inclusion if we can justify preparing students to become clerks and perhaps merchants. We can also justify its inclusion if we can show that we then make students better able to live in a world governed by money and other basic qualifications. But no one of these reasons has much weight for one who is essentially occupied with properly satisfying the present need of the child to understand and to live in its world, and its right to move to the stage where it will be a vital youth.

We cannot defend the teaching of arithmetic to children solely on the ground that their wits will be sharpened as a consequence. It is doubtful whether skills mastered in one field can be used effectively in others. And in any case, arithmetic is a subject which can be mastered without much straining of the intellect, even the intellect of a backward child—a fact which will not be evident so long as arithmetic is confused with mathematics. Arithmetic is little more than a set of simple rules to be learned through memorization, and then applied repetitively in situation after situation. We know now that problems which can be solved by arithmetical means can be dealt with more accurately and more rapidly by machines. Why should we teach the child what can be done better by a machine?

The teaching of arithmetic can be justified in the same way and to the same degree that we can justify the teaching of vocabulary, spelling, and pronunciation. All are useful means. They make it easier to proceed with the more important work of learning how to use the body and mind creatively, with some sense of what they are and can do and what their success and failure import for man.

The child should know how to reason well. It should accept and make use of long-lived truths and large generalities. It deserves to be taught how to observe accurately and how to use abstractions effectively. We want it to acquire habits of precision, and to learn how to reach desired results along alternative routes. But this means that we are to teach it not only arithmetic but mathematics, not only vocabulary but reading, not only spelling but writing, not only pronunciation but speech. These lead to the envisagement of the universal and abstract, and a confrontation of the important. All learning requires the exercise of self-discipline and the use of creative powers, thereby enabling the child to entertain new possibilities for thought and action which bring it to the edge of the world about to be.

8]

Every society has its own code of proper and improper attitudes and behavior. This is largely conventional and traditional, and is rarely made explicit. Difficult to alter, it is not to be violated with impunity.

A mixture of social law and social manners, the social code expresses the viable morality of a people. Even more than speech this morality is often taken to be sufficiently well-inculcated, in an informal way, in the course of familial and social life. But unless deliberate attention is given to the virtue of respecting the rights of others, what is informally taught will be largely routine acts backed by approved gestures and postures.

Virtues are most effectively infused in and utilized by the child through participation in simple games. Here, in the course of the production of a common course of action, the child learns to share in the school spirit. Unknowingly, it thereby acquires the virtues of loyalty and cooperation, and incidentally achieves something of a center in itself in relation to other equally real and important centers.

Games entrain rivalries and competition. These are not altogether evil, particularly if they are nothing more than the inevitable outcome of the expression of an antecedent solidarity with a group. Allowed to dominate, allowed to become the primary objective of the game, competition will feed the vices of conceit, pride, and intolerance, or their equally regrettable counterparts, lack of confidence, shame, and obstinacy. Most educators are acutely aware of these dangers and try to minimize them. But those educators at the same time also actively increase them when they insist on the use of examinations, with the consequent grading of students in relation to one another.

Devices for determining whether something has been taught, and to what extent, have a place in an educational system, particularly in a mobile society where we are forced to decide quickly how to place and how to teach new students. But the examinations should then be taken, not to offer exhibits of what has been mastered, but as tests in which the student can effectively and creatively utilize, *put to the test*, what he has learned. Used to provide exhibits of what had been memorized or had become habitual, examinations will tell us more about the character of the teaching than about the character of the student and what he has in fact made his own. Marks are, at best, boundaries below which the student can be seen not to have fallen. They do not and cannot tell what the learning means to him in mind, body, or spirit, and thus whether he has been educated or not.

Schools offer a time and a place where one can be free from a concern with immediate practical affairs. No matter how much work the school demands of the child, the child lives in a leisured world. But a leisured world is not a world that can be properly punctuated by examinations, quantified, subdivided, and organized in terms of indices of one's ability to make evident how many detached items of information he has readily available.

A beginning chess player attends to the rules; a master concentrates on the moves. For good teachers the master chess player is a fellow spirit, even though he is not concerned with the moves of living beings. Perhaps an even closer fellow spirit is a cook, particularly as contrasted with a baker. A baker's desirable results are predictable and endlessly duplicable, but the cook improvises. His recipes are general guides which, while well tested, are to be specified and even modified in the light of the available ingredients and the circumstances. A good teacher also finds flexible ways in which to use methods that have been long tried and widely accepted.

9]

The well-taught child has been taught to be a child. Through the help of story, it has been made aware of a realm of importance where abiding truths intersect the actual course of the world. In its play and in its work it comes more and more to focus on those truths and becomes better adjusted to the world as it is evidenced now in the presence and activities of fellow children and the teacher. Dealt with sympathetically, guided but not driven, helped to utilize whatever native powers it has, the child is able to develop and use other powers.

Over the course of the decade the child's size and shape undergo considerable alteration. There is a marked increase in its dexterity and in its capacity to exercise self-control. During that time it may lose interest in learning; its attention may flag, its curiosity vanish, it may become lax and indifferent. In good health, it might achieve a good youthful body, but this will exhibit only childish ideas and childish ways. Why is this? The dominant theories either suppose that the limit of the child's abilities have been reached, or that a natural and otherwise inevitable maturation has been blocked by incompetent teaching. The first of these views tacitly supposes that the child has been taught as well as it can be taught. But most teaching is not of a high order. And because children come from diverse backgrounds and all have had different experiences, whatever is taught to all will differ in availability and value from child to child. The other view is a little better. But it supposes that good teaching is a sovereign remedy. Good teaching is not quite that. The best of teachers have not succeeded in holding the attention or in sustaining the development of some promising students.

The problem is in part one of native equipment. Some minds are unfortunately overlimited. They cannot be made to operate on material which is within the capacity of children of about the same age. But even among children with the same capacities there is a difference. Some are alert and some are not, some try where others relax. Children differ in character and in motivation.

Everyone, child or adult, at every moment is faced with the need to advance or to retreat, or to maintain his ground. At every moment each must decide whether to continue, to stop, or to change his ways. Whatever he does may end in satisfaction or frustration, in reward or punishment, in pleasure or pain. And wherever he ends, what he obtains may be enough for him, or be something to be merely possessed and then passed beyond.

In many cases we can help the child to decide in ways which will help it prosper, particularly if the issues are familiar and large-sized. But there are many new situations, and many cases which are almost too small for anyone—even the most attentive of teachers—to notice. As a consequence a child is forced to risk again and again. The decisions it then makes, half-consciously, make no small difference to the character it forges.

Curiosity tempts the child to advance into new territory. But it can advance too soon and too far. Frustrations and defeats will then tempt it to be more cautious in the future. The caution may be excessive, with the consequence that the child may stay within too small a region and be willing thereafter to adventure in only a few cases. From the very beginning it should have been taught, in idealized, controlled situations, that different topics make different demands and involve different risks. It must learn that there is an equilibrium point where it can attain maximum benefit with least danger. Gradually habits of sound discrimination, sensible estimation, and good judgment must be built up to turn it into a reasonable child, at home in its world.

The defeats the child suffered in the past make it stop at a place where another might have advanced. Were the child not supported by its teachers, did it not have inspiring examples before it, it would have stopped earlier than it did. But in the end it must decide for itself, and in that decision take the first step toward forging a life style. No one can tell in advance how the child will decide in the new cases it constantly confronts. Operating under the influence of the character it has achieved, it must now exercise its will in order to determine that character along old or new lines. Its life is constantly in the making, and no one knows how it will be made. No educational scheme or practice can save the child from the need or desirability of having to make its own decisions, and thereby express and make its own personality. It is helped to do this when the general principles of the educational process are quickened by sympathetic teachers who have won the child's trust.

The educational process should respect the differences that exist among children. It should never slide over the truth that each child is unique. Still it can never go much beyond enabling all to achieve large-scale results—right habits, sound principles, good judgment, desirable character, and an entrance into another, more complex world. By the time the child reaches adolescence it should begin to have an interest in the prospects, challenges, and rewards of the youth.

Youth is the inheritance of a matured child, of a child who, while being satisfied as a child, stretches to what lies just beyond its reach. If the child has not come this far, there is nothing better to do than to retrace the steps by which it came to its present impasse. We must go back to the point where the child lost its trust in others and in itself, and there help it to try again to get an appropriate fulfillment. It must then be encouraged to make another effort toward the attainment of a wider, richer, or even just a newer satisfaction. A return will then have been made to the work of completing the education of the child and getting it readied for its life as a youth.

The primary school awakens and encourages curiosity; it also inculcates habits expressive of a respect for authority, thereby giving form and direction to the immature. From good primary school training a youth should emerge who has some skill in the use, conservation, and development of the material and spiritual resources of the society. It is the task of the secondary school to take that youth and turn him into a young man.

2

The Tween-Age

THERE IS NO HARDER PROBLEM in education than to know how to satisfy and dissatisfy the student at the same time. The solution is easy to conceive and say, but very hard to produce in fact: the student must be taught in the proper spirit. A child's studies should not, obviously, be beyond the reach of its abilities. It is no less obvious, even though more often overlooked, that the child deserves satisfactions appropriate to its abilities. It must make use of its powers, but in such a way as to quicken a drive to leave its child-life behind. It must be taught only what it can master, but in such a way that it comes to master something else.

The content that can be mastered properly at one stage of a career is too formidable for an earlier stage and too elementary for a later. If what is mastered at the earlier stage is to make possible a mastery at the later, the child's appetite for what is to come must be aroused. Successful teaching changes the child to make it one who wants to be taught something else, and who ought to be taught in a spirit which should be in consonance with the disposition of the child and the nature of the subject.

Children can be taught by fine and dedicated teachers and yet be unable to learn because they are not yet ready to master the content which is being presented to them. As a consequence they become bewildered and discouraged.

Children might be well-grounded in the elements of a subject and therefore be well-prepared to deal with more difficult branches of it, but they may nevertheless be unable to benefit from the spirit in which that more difficult material is properly taught. They thereupon become disheartened and perhaps humiliated. In both ways the children lose interest in the very topics for which they had been partly prepared in content or in attitude.

Were biological growth the inescapable outcome of some ennobling power, irresistibly bringing the child to higher and higher levels, teaching would not be a very difficult matter. The teacher would merely have to satisfy the student at a particular stage of his career and then wait for the next stage to arrive, when the student is to be satisfied in a new, appropriate way. But instead we must ready the child for new content and new teaching.

Biological growth provides new channels for and new amounts of energy, but by itself it cannot enable one to learn more difficult material, nor does it prepare one to have it taught from a new position. There is little warrant for the hope that old interests will decay with time and that desirable new ones will inevitably take their place. No one has a reservoir of unfailing energy and desire. Students do not run into the vacuum of ignorance with new, driving, and appropriate concerns. All must be helped to receive more advanced material and to deal with it properly.

If a student is not satisfied at each stage of his career, his life becomes tedious and his school a burden. And if he is not lured into unsuspected fields he will circle about that from which he should have departed. Students must be lured while they are enriched, satisfied while they are being tempted to move on. In the very act of being fulfilled they must be led forward; while moving on they must benefit from what they have been taught. At one and the same time they must be in equilibrium and in disequilibrium, quieted and restless, fulfilled and unfulfilled. They must learn that what they have mastered leaves them still incomplete; they must become aware that they need and really want something more. Dissatisfaction should environ every student's satisfactions.

The proper teaching of a subject leads a student to become interested in learning something which is at present outside the scope of his concepts and capacities. Poetry, for example, properly taught awakens an alertness to the value of language, grammar, civilization, and religion. It makes the student aware of the tragedy and comedy of existence, of which poems are both epitomizations and revelations. Mathematics properly taught awakens a concern for precision, rules, and proofs, and provides some inkling of the reality and nature of abiding truths. The proper teaching of science builds up an interest in theories and laws, and conveys something of the cut of the cosmos in which we live.

The good teacher is alert to the fact that students are sensitive and unsure, that they have little experience and large areas of ignorance, that they are parts of a distinctive world, and that they are inescapably conditioned and perhaps flawed by what happened to them earlier. The better his teaching, the more will a topic be grasped by the student as pointing beyond itself. To point to something is of course not yet to arrive at it. Not only must direction be given; the student must be helped to move on to satisfy that part of his newly awakened appetite which nothing in the present could wholly satisfy.

2]

Like philosophy, education begins in wonder. It too starts with the awareness that something is not altogether intelligible or complete, and that it is worth the full effort of a man to make it so. But though what is known provides indications of how and by what it is to be made intelligible or complete, no child or young person is able to provide it. They are not able to move on much beyond the point where they now are unless they receive help. Parents and teachers must make them aware of the values which are latent in the subject matter of which they have only a partial grasp. If the student is not properly guided, what he has not yet mastered will easily become the idle object of random fancies rather than the proper topic of a sustained interest.

The guidance usually given, for the most part, reflects the current values or myths of the society. It wants the home and the school to live up to the society's standards, actual or hoped for—usually hoped for. But since even the best of societies can be criticized with justice, and since there are goods beyond the interest and reach of any and every society, parent and teacher must defy the society to some extent, or fail in their purpose.

The task of the school is to teach the student to try to realize ideals more comprehensive and fundamental than those which are usually socially cherished. So far as the school has public support it is, of course, subject to public inspection and public conditions. As part of the society, it has to conform to the mores and the laws. But for its own good, and for the good of its charges, the society should allow the school its freedom. It should take the school to have a reality and a being of its own, pointing the new generation to a new world which, while continuing the present, goes beyond it.

School is society's way of making society better, by directing students to truths and values not now enjoyed, cherished, or perhaps known. It should not be viewed, as Dewey does, as an agency for preserving the values of the society. At the very best, school is a means by which those values are focused on in order to be transmitted and *transformed*.

3]

The advocates of educational methods tend to suppose that they are going in the right direction—
even those who explicitly affirm that there is no right direction, or no way of knowing what it is. The supposition
is not credible. But even if it were, there would be no justification for educational theory to be so absorbed, as it now
is, in the problem of method with its accompanying psychology of learning. He who concentrates on these may
perhaps learn to teach, but he will not learn to learn.
Teachers need to learn content as well as methods. And
they should be taught that even the best of methods offers
only a technique whose value is to be determined by seeing
whether or not in living practice it enables students to be
creative and efficient, to learn and to advance, to master
and to be prepared to learn more.

A good teacher uses a number of methods in the course
of his day, depending on what best enables him to convey
content and importance, fact and value, and the past, present, and future. He is most effective when governed by a
strong desire to teach and when he has learned how to
interplay with his students in the course of their process of
learning. Yet when one considers the vexations, the petty
rules of institutions of learning, and the narrow vision of
administrators; when one compares the social status, financial rewards, and responsibilities of teachers with those
that are characteristic of others who are less well-equipped,
less devoted, and less intelligent, it is hard to escape won-
derment at the fact that anyone is willing to teach—particularly those who are eminently qualified.

Why should a man become a teacher? Is it because he
likes to help the young? Usually. Is it because he likes to
find out something about himself? Sometimes. Is it because

he likes to discover something for himself? Often. Is it because he learns? Yes, that is evidently the strongest of his motives. Until it comes to the fore the teacher will most likely fail to be the teacher he ought to be.

The teacher of reading and writing brings the child into contact with the simplest words and structures; these are enough to give the teacher an experience of grammar *in concreto*, and a better awareness of the mystery and glory of language. The teaching of mathematics brings the child into contact with general rules and abstract concepts; it reveals to the alert teacher the way in which general truths are embodied in limited contexts. He will benefit the student but little, however, and gain nothing for himself if he does not himself exhibit the virtues of honesty, kindness, and discipline, or if he does not keep alive in himself and his students the sense of wonder and the joy of discovery. Articulating and sympathizing, the teacher inevitably gives new value to his own knowledge and experience; inevitably he educates himself.

There has, of course, never been a teacher so noble. But then there never was a student who could maximally benefit from him. Students on the whole deserve better teachers than they often get, but that is quite another thing from saying that they deserve to have teachers who are better than any teachers have ever been. Students and teachers both have defects. But there is no reason why these should not be reduced in number and effect.

Education is the coming together of those who know and those who are ignorant, of older and younger, of the bearer of a message and the uninformed. The teacher himself is also ignorant; he too is a learner. The student in turn is his teacher's teacher; he reveals what the impact of knowledge is on innocence, what effect honesty and competence, friendliness intertwined with dignity, have on the outlook of the young. By guiding the student toward fulfillment the teacher incidentally learns something of the nature of freshness, creativity, and growth.

The object of teaching is the making of men. This requires that great goods be given limited forms, and that these, under ideal conditions, be made the individual's own. Education prepares the individual for the eventual, maximum achievement of those goods, under the actual conditions of daily life.

4]

The educated man has been prepared to live a full life. Since a full life takes account of every dimension of knowledge, being, and value, education apparently gives him a mastery in the concrete of what philosophy understands in the abstract. It is philosophy made practical, philosophy lived through. To see this most clearly account should be taken of the fact that good educational theory begins not at one but at two ends.

There is a final end that should be reached by all. That end should guide the reflections and evaluations, the course and the decisions of educational theory and practice. But educational theory must also take account of what has been learned. It should attend to the start of the educational venture at every level of the individual's career. The two ends together make evident that sound educational theory uses the funded wisdom of the past to make possible the achievement of maximum good for man. An education which ignores this goal would not move where it should. We all aim at something not yet possessed; we all use what had been acquired in the past. If we do not keep clear what lies in front and behind we will aim where and preserve what we ought not.

No man can free himself from his culture or his background. No one can entirely ignore all the lessons of the past; the most one could do in that direction would be to make surreptitious, nonsystematic, and usually improper use of them. Everyone of us is a child of his tradition. That tradition is transmitted through the teacher's learning and skills, backed by his character and personality. Through his power, students' capacities are forged into habits, and ignorance gives place to knowledge. It is the teacher who helps those in the present to absorb and preserve what was valuable in the past.

At every stage the student must learn how to become more and more self-reliant, more and more at the center of himself, more and more a person, fulfilled in a world where other individuals are equally well-fulfilled. This does not preclude the teaching of common subjects in a common way to a number of students at the same time, provided that what is taught is allowed to be received in distinctive individual ways.

The good life is one in which an individual is qualified to make personally relevant evaluations and decisions on vitally important topics. But before that goal is reached he must learn how to use what is taught, and learn how to teach himself. The highest reaches of education are outside the grasp of those who do not engage in a process of self-education, who do not adopt the role of both teacher and student. No one is finally educated who does not subject himself to constant and searching self-reflection and self-criticism. The ground for this is laid in the proper teaching of the child.

5]

The child's life spans about a decade. It will take another decade before we can be confident that the child has arrived at the point where it can become a mature man. That decade readily breaks into two almost equal parts. The first is the period of youth. It runs from adolescence to about eighteen—when the youth is thought fit to drive, to be a soldier, to earn a living, to marry, and perhaps to drink. That this is a singular period is now widely known. It has even acquired a distinctive but misleading name, "the teen-age." That name leads one to suppose that the period embraces all those who are in their teens. But a thirteen-year-old is still a child, and a nineteen-year-old is often a young man, at the beginning of the second half of the decade which ends with the arrival of a man. To avoid slipping into the supposition that a nineteen-year-old belongs to the same culture or requires the same type of education as a thirteen- or even a seventeen-year-old, it would be better to give this first half of the decade, following on childhood, another name. Since it comes after childhood but before the time that one can be properly called a "young man" it would not be altogether inappropriate to call it the "tween-age." All ages, of course, except the very first and last, are between others, but none, I think, so evidently shows the marks of where it had issued from and into what it will pass as this period of some five years.

The second half of the second decade is the age of the young man. For five years, more or less, he will live the life of an apprentice to living. His formal schooling will be devoted to bringing him in contact with the basic disciplines, the main life-styles, and the achievements and promise of civilization. Hopefully, he will undergo a long, slow process of maturation, to arrive at the position where he is able to spend the rest of his days as a ripened, wise, and decent man. But the ground for this has to be well-laid much earlier.

6]

The child acts with spontaneity, without much forethought and without express goal. The youth tends to act on impulse—spontaneity channelized and directed at some end. The child's mind and will, its emotions, and bodily movements are not sharply distinguished or capable of functioning in much independence of one another. It lacks well-defined routes of expression. It cannot, for any appreciable period, exercise some one power while suppressing the others. Making use of one power, its energies and attention spill over so that it is also involved with the others. The youth in contrast with the child has better defined organs and muscles, greater critical powers, and is better able to control his mind and body. In part because he has been trained and taught properly, and in part because he has undergone biological development, he can exercise his different powers without necessarily affecting others. He can think without desiring, desire without lusting, lust without willing, will without intending, and intend without acting. The educational task is to correct rather than to direct him, to stabilize rather than to encourage him, to adapt him rather than to sustain him.

The child has no sure way of moving in and through itself, or in and through the world about. It is effectively isolated until family and teacher help it make contact with the larger world. It needs support in the shape of sympathy; it must learn to trust others; it must be willing to risk exposing its delicate self to a larger and impersonal, and apparently ruthless and irrational world. The youth neither needs nor can make good use of sympathy. He already is part of the world, and is somewhat adept at using some of its major roads. He is sustained, not by trust, but by a confidence in himself and others, and by an awareness that others do and can count on him. What he wants and needs, and can make good use of, is kindness. And if we are to be most kind to him we must accept him with his weaknesses and strengths, while granting him the dignity of being responsible for what he does.

The child has not earned the right to be responsible, but it has a right to be held accountable. The one attributes a fault, the other a defect. Responsibility presupposes knowledge and control, accountability requires only the capacity to be corrected and improved. The child is not responsible because it has no power to bring a knowledge of right and wrong into effective play. Because it has only a thin and fluctuating knowledge of good and evil, it is not morally to blame. It may be wicked, but it is never guilty because its intentions do not have objectives which it can by itself attain. The child though is accountable for what it does, and is to be reproved, corrected, redirected, and shamed for regrettable acts which have their origin or their mainspring in it.

The youth is responsible. He is worthy of being criticized, condemned, or praised, as one who does some things intentionally, aware of what is right and wrong. At the same time he is to be held accountable for signal failures to fit inside the public domain. The kindness which he needs in order to be properly taught is based on a respect for him as a responsible and accountable being. It encourages him to function in his tween-age world without the need to break society's rules and suffer its punishments.

A society has characteristic patterns which the youth must be taught to respect and of which he has to learn to partake. He must come to know its values and its achievements. In school, and to a lesser degree at home and in the community, he should be taught to belong to his society, but not at the sacrifice of the powers he has or of their proper youthful use.

Tween-agers have always been in rebellion against the established ways. There is some justification for this. Most of these ways are conventional, many are arbitrary, and some are foolish or irrational. In the past, though, the tween-age rebellion against them has been episodic, sullen, and mainly subterranean; today it is rather steady, sometimes organized, and rather vociferous. The change is partly due to the fact that the rightful demands of society (which is, after all, a society for the old as well as the young, for the future as well as for the present) have been urged without adequate regard for the rights and sensibility of youths. Not yet ready to be a full part of society, they are nevertheless held responsible and accountable by and to it. Half citizens, with more energy and less control than their elders, they form a subculture which is not altogether in gear with other subcultures involving other age groups.

The child finds it hard to achieve a proper balance between its desires and what it ought in fact to desire and obtain. It must be taught temperance. The youth instead must be taught the virtue of courage, where this is understood to be (as Plato long ago observed) the knowledge of what to fear. A courageous man has the habit of placing himself squarely before the demands of evil and attending to the demands of the good. That habit is best acquired in youth through the practice of small acts, not necessarily threatening to life or limb, but which nevertheless allow for a shock to self-esteem and cherished values. Youth is the time when one sets out to meet the challenges of the world, but under the protection of wise and experienced councilors. None will ever be as kind again as those encountered in a good school—or as badly needed.

The child is taught through story and the specializations this promotes. It learns neither particulars nor universals; instead it achieves a general outlook and acquires some skill in finding its way about in a world which this outlook pervades. The education of the youth pays more attention to particulars and the kind of universals these display. The items he studies are to be mastered by distinctive activities which are governed by a regard for the implications that the universals sustain.

The adventures of gods, princes, and fairies intrigue the child; the youth instead attends to idealized but authentic tales of great good and bad men, of true heroism and cowardice. He does not identify himself with those whom he admires; rather he takes them to be models and sources of inspiration, part of a relevant past. The lesson he needs and wants to learn is that there once had been large-sized men who struggled nobly and successfully with the basic issues that every man must confront in a brute and often cruel world.

Accounts of great adventures, discoveries, and crises convey to the youth the kind of ideals that should be realized, and which have sometimes in fact been realized, and are still realizable. But he does not attend primarily to these. His attention is focused on the men who embody those ideals and who have made their power felt. It is these whom he takes to be his ancestors; it is their role he would assume and their solutions and successes he would duplicate if he could. He is therefore ready to be challenged again and again in mind and in body. To teach him well we need but repeat in miniature, within the school setting, the heroic world to which he wants to belong.

The tween-ager must be taught specific things, trained in special skills, for the challenges of the world which are never general must be met by grand thoughts and ardent desires. Mathematics, history, literature, physical training, the mastery of intellectual and other tools, the working of modern machinery all require that he learn how to restrain his impulses, and acquire the appropriate skills.

Because the child's spontaneity is too episodic, unstructured, and unfocused to allow it to be expressed in the form in which it initially appears, it must be constantly structured and restructured, to help the child be in a position where it will gain by being free. The child achieves its maximum freedom when it is denied liberty, the privilege of doing what it likes. The youth rightly takes and is granted greater liberties than the child. He is therefore able to learn the values and responsibilities of being free. Over the course of his career his wit and judgment are sharpened; slowly he builds up a fund of reliable knowledge; gradually he carves out a distinctive life-style, and learns who he is and what he can do.

The child is beset by fears, threats, and dangers; again and again it loses hope and direction. But if it is watched and sympathized with, its failures will not usually grow large in size or number. This does not preclude the child's escape into its own recesses because it has exaggerated the risks it now confronts or the losses it has suffered. Considerable sympathy and the promise of protection may be required before it will adventure out again. But the youth neither gets nor wants such sympathy or protection. He needs and wants guidance and criticism. When he retreats, it is usually not toward his privacy but toward some other area where he can function better than he had before. Where the child adventures as one ready to retreat into its secret self, the youth adventures as one ready to adventure once again in a new direction.

The child is a natural but momentary monist, ready to absorb what it encounters into what is at the forefront of its attention. The youth instead is a natural and occasional realist, trying to do justice for a period now to this task and then to that. To be most successful he must learn how to maximize his powers and master the use of them separately and together.

7]

The child comes to the close of its decade able to do a number of things involving the use of distinctive organs and abilities. Its body has increased in size; various appetites, particularly the sexual, come raging to the fore. Increased strength adds fuel, and gives new importance to his emotions, allowing them a more sustained and vigorous expression over a larger area. The youth is subject to still greater bodily demands. His appetites and emotions do not merely come to the surface; they grip him, they upset him, they drive him. He must protect himself— his hardest and most important job. He must learn to deliberate and choose what before he neither noted nor could deal with. And when he does, he and others will become more and more aware that he is a singular individual with a distinctive ego, the nature of which, though still obscure, is made more and more evident in his speech and in his acts.

Like the child the youth also lives in a world of his own. We did not have to wait for educational geniuses—as we did in the case of the child—to make us aware of this fact. It is too strongly insisted on by the youth. But educators tend to misconstrue the world of the youth. They take it to be charged with defiance, threatening the stability of the adult world. They meet the supposed challenge with discipline and punishment, corporal and otherwise, with the primary purpose of keeping the youth subdued. Only youth properly cowed, it has been thought, is ready for a training which would make him acceptable to higher institutions of learning. But what is needed and what is deserved is an intelligent, considerate concern for the youth and his present problems.

The youth needs education in the difficult work of trying to find himself. He must be helped to be himself, and to protect himself. Despite his moods, his discontinuity in idea and work, despite his confusions and contradictions, he knows what he admires and therefore what he would like to be. But he does not know how to reach his goal, particularly in the face of the violent impulses that tear through him despite all his efforts at self-control.

The youth is more habituated than the child, and stronger too, but still somewhat pliable and unformed. Left to himself he indulges one ability or power, sometimes for a moment and sometimes for too long a time, and then switches to others without rationale or justification. As a consequence, he tends to exaggerate one side of his nature, or allows many sides to develop haphazardly and inadequately. In the first way he makes more difficult a harmonization of his different channels and achievements; in the second he fails to exercise his capacities correctly or to the full. It is one of the functions of the school to help him do justice to his many sides by making him deal with specific problems in the classroom and on the playground. It must help him learn to accept himself somewhat the way in which adults must learn to accept the child. This means that, among other things, he must be made aware that his rights and freedom are to be uniquely expressed by him in a world where others are engaged in equally unique and justified expressions.

8]

Education is not only occupied with ideas and concepts, with information and theories. It helps build character and enables the child to become part of a traditionalized state of affairs. The school of which the child makes use is a formal, idealized, foreshortened setting in which the student can become more mature, more aware, more civilized. To bring it where it ought to be, the school simplifies, purifies, and extends the student's natural interests. Eventually the school will come to the end of its own resources. Eventually it will define itself to be no longer necessary or desirable for those whom it has in its care. Its greatest achievement is to get the student to the stage where he is prepared to leave it, willing to function as a self-possessed man, able to work out his destiny inside the hardly discernible but almost unbreakable boundaries of his society and his daily world.

We all need instruments and occasions for the effective exercise of our powers, for the evaluation of what there is, and for the participation, both actively and passively, in all that has been achieved in being and knowledge. These the school can provide. It can offer the youth both a training in the art of living and a laboratory where he can experiment, with little danger and much profit, on that little bud, his tender self. It is the school that enables him to become independent, intellectually and personally, by helping him to become more perceptive, both aesthetically and humanly, and to become more receptive to the ideas, values, and aims of others. It sees to it that students share in common ideals and make use of common knowledge as creative, sensitive persons. Its hope is that they will eventually be enriched, private individuals who live together without undue friction in a common society and world.

The secondary school encourages and satisfies those secondary appetites and interests which become manifest when the student has passed beyond the boundaries of childhood. Its concern is with those matters of importance which can be enjoyed by youths who are capable of assuming the responsibility for being a part of a traditionalized world.

By subdividing and departmentalizing its curriculum the secondary school is able to promote an understanding of the processes and temper of the community; it can help the youth develop good habits of discourse, and encourage his enjoyment of the arts. But there ought also to be activities and subjects having an integrative function, making evident that there is a common body of knowledge and a common spirit behind the human endeavor to know and to serve. This is best done when the secondary school keeps in focus the meaning of the crucial events of life in that society—birth, sickness, love, marriage, war, and death—and the great achievements of mankind in creation, adventure, and discovery which still have some bearing on what now occurs. Literature, history, and a participation in basic scientific approaches are excellent means now used in many places for just these purposes.

Human happiness is in part a consequence of the satisfaction of large areas of a man's need to know and to create. If a school will teach students to read with understanding and to think with feeling it will provide the necessary tools for this. Strictly speaking, the secondary school provides a vocational training in the art of becoming a flexible, maturing person. Concentrating on enabling the tween-agers to find a place for themselves in relation to others, it enables them to become more reasonable. This is important work. But the growth of popular education has come to mean that the secondary school is no longer at the heart of American education. The stress has shifted toward college. Nevertheless, no matter how much our colleges expand, they will not provide the main education of the vast majority of men, for there is a restlessness in the young which makes it hard for them to stay in school much past eighteen. The secondary school would be wise to give some thought to this. It should prepare youths in such a way that though they do not go to college, they are able to continue their education outside school and eventually live full lives. Only if it does this can we be confident that a large body of the population will not remain radically unfulfilled.

The child's incapacity to interest itself for long in any enterprise precludes its exclusive occupation with its body. Because the youth has the ability to concentrate, he, in contrast, can spend more time than he should on bodily matters. His explorations of his body are no longer as idle and as innocent as they were before. He may spend a great deal of energy and time in bodily activities with the result that he often is too fatigued to be able to interest himself in any other kind. He must engage in controlled exercise, not solely to promote the virtue of courage or to produce a healthy body, but also to enable his body to be developed in the best possible way, consistent with the best possible use of his diverse powers. His abilities and potentialities must be allowed development; otherwise he will continue to be immature.

The school should encourage the achievement of a well-functioning totality. It ought not only to help minds to grow, but through contests with nature and through games and sports it should teach the tween-ager how to possess and use his body. The world of game and sport is a tiny copy of the larger world. Here one can work together with others; here one can benefit from what the rest do; here one can become an individual alongside others. The world of game and sport teaches the tween-ager what he is and what he can do with and over against the realities around him. It helps give him a sense of achievement, and it helps him to grow in confidence and self-control.

Coaches have succeeded in helping youths to a degree

others can only envy and try to imitate. But coaches must sometimes be reminded that the world of game and sport does not encompass all that is valuable. It does not offer the best or the only places where emotions and minds are to be challenged, tested, and improved; it does not even take care of every rightful demand of the body, for some techniques and skills—careful measurement, reading, and writing—are mastered only in the laboratory or classroom.

9]

The youth must be taught the proper use of his emotions. Too little expression of the emotions ends with the arid and remote; too much ends with the confused and distraught. A proper expression of the emotions is achieved by getting the youth involved in arts and crafts, both as a spectator and as a practitioner. He will then be able to express his emotions in a controlled and ordered way, no longer allowing them to explode without benefit to himself or anyone else. If he engages in a making, directed at producing the excellent, his emotions are spelled out and spent in the course of the production.

One way of encouraging tween-agers to engage in the arts and crafts and to enjoy them, is by getting them to read histories and romantic literature. Another is by having them visit museums and galleries. A third is by having them engage in a direct experimental exploration of various techniques and media. If the arts and crafts are to be well-mastered through the proper use of the emotions, all three routes will have to be followed.

No youth has the experience or knowledge, and thus the capacity, to properly examine and evaluate works of art. His natural interest and bent will have to be gradually corrected before he is able to judge wisely and well. To help him here better and richer works must be substituted for those which he initially prefers.

Education is the correction of the bad taste of students.

To begin with, that taste is vagrant, rough, a testimony only to what immediately pleases or displeases. It must be improved, made to give way to a sensitive discrimination, alert to nuances and the effect of the whole on the parts and the parts on the whole.

The arts and crafts are difficult fields in which to be at ease. Because much preparation and hard work is required to make a reasonable beginning in them, some educators are tempted to ignore those arts and crafts which do not seem to be vocationally or economically viable. They prefer those that require only a minimal amount of self-discipline and little time. But there are no such arts or crafts.

One can justify the teaching of needlework, carpentry, clay modeling, group singing, and the writing of simple autobiographies as means for sharpening discrimination, for learning the texture of different materials, for promoting the exercise of the imagination, and for stimulating cooperation. But it would be a mistake to conclude that one has then mastered an art or a craft. Art is the making of the beautiful, an excellent finality; craft is the making of the graceful, an excellent means. It takes years of concentrated concern before a man can be said to have become a genuine practitioner of either.

The arts and crafts are more than occasions for the controlled expression of the emotions. Indeed, they will never be properly pursued until they are taken account of in their own terms. The youth is not yet able to do this. But he can be taught the rudiments of various arts and crafts; his senses and imagination can be satisfied in such a way as to make him ready to give himself later to the production of the excellent. He can be taught how to use his emotions as agencies for sharpening his sense of what it means to exist in a world with others, all sharing the same past and desiring more or less the same goods. If he can gain some insight into the world which he shares with his ancestors, he will be better prepared to contribute to or to properly enjoy the arts and crafts later on.

Great ventures, terrible trials of strength and endurance, exhibitions of bravery, sacrifice and devotion, brighten the world of youth. Noble deeds make him aware, not of the nature of politics or history (of which he has little understanding and in which he has little interest), but of the nature of man at his best in relation to fellowman and nature. This he wants to understand, and this he is now capable of learning. His task is to realize in his own context, through an active facing of appropriate physical and mental challenges, the glories that have already excited his spirit.

There are those who would not have the young read about wars. War is always regrettable, always to be looked at with dismay and horror. On this almost all men are agreed. No one should speak of war in laudatory terms, even as providing an occasion for great feats, unusual courage, and desirable victories. If we could justify such speaking we would be also warranted, when teaching the child, to speak favorably of the wicked stepmother on the ground that she makes possible the adventures and the success of the good prince.

Wars interest the young. In ways that the young can both understand and feel, wars make vivid signal tensions and crises, exhibiting the vigorous action that is needed if defeat and frustration are to be overcome. There is a point then in a teaching focused on wars, particularly those of one's own nation, but only if these provide occasions for the exhibition of extreme instances of the ways men faced and should face dangerous forces. The constant temptation to glorify a war, particularly when it ends in a victory for the right, can be at least partly overcome by focusing on the character of the men involved, and particularly those who have exercised heroic virtues for the benefit of others. This is consistent with the refusal to condone the war's destructiveness and injustices. If it is a blunder to avoid showing the young the times and occasions when men are severely tried, it is no less a blunder to transfer the nobility of men to the wars in which they fought.

Today many are asking whether religion should be

taught in the secondary schools. Unfortunately the question is not very clear. If by religion we mean the distinct creeds, each with its claim to be alone supremely mature and completely acceptable to God, the answer must surely be in the negative. To favor one creed over another is to go directly counter to the Constitution. Yet if we try to deal with them all neutrally, as on the same level of value and truth, despite each one's direct denial that the others are in as sound a position as it is, we will teach not religion but a way of taking a nonreligious attitude toward the various creeds, and will end by making the different religious claims appear implausible or extravagant.

Teachers should not only avoid encouraging belligerence or endorsing wars, they must also avoid defending particular religions and religious outlooks. But they can make intelligible the nature of religious choice and life. It is desirable, I think, for the teacher to make evident the glory of charity and of service on behalf of mankind—virtues which are traditionally oriented in a religion, and are perhaps never pursued with enthusiasm apart from it. The religious leader can be presented as being something like a hero, a splendid, inspiring part of the youth's inheritance. Because religion is a dimension of the tradition which the youth is to make his own, it has a place in the history that is taught in the secondary school.

10]

Helped to have a sound body and to make good use of it, the tween-ager must also be helped to have a mind. That mind will be superior to that of the child's. Why is this so? No good reasons are immediately apparent. Once again, it must be emphasized that mere increase in age does not provide a sufficient explanation. If it did, we would have no need to educate at all, and could just wait for a sufficient time to pass until the child automatically acquired a first-rate mind operating at its best. Nor does biological growth offer a sufficient explanation. If it did, the mind would be mainly or entirely a function of the body, and all we would have to do in order to improve the mind would be to improve the body. But there are men with strong, good bodies who have weak, poor minds, and men with fine minds whose bodies are inferior to most.

A youthful mind is one that had been active in a child. That child has already had experience in the art of inferring correctly, and has some sense of the kind of relevance some items have to others. The mind of the youth builds on the knowledge and makes use of the abilities acquired by the child. It is a mind that has already attained some degree of reasonableness and must now be taught to be rational as well.

To be reasonable is to know what is usually expected to follow upon what is now confronted. To be rational is to know what must follow, no matter what is usually expected; it is to be keyed to the rationale of different objects and subject matters. The rational mind follows rules; it is guided by principles; it submits to laws having a role inside what is known. Rarely does the youth know such rules, principles, or laws. When explicitly stated they assume for him the guise of mnemonic devices or dried formulae. Fortunately, he need not know them in order to be able to reason properly, any more than a swimmer need know the laws of hydrodynamics or the chemistry of the muscles in order to be able to speed through the water.

Without losing his reasonableness, the youth must learn to be rational. If we offer him rules, we offer what to him can be only empty abstractions. If we sink him into specific subjects as they are in fact dealt with by adults, we drown him in details. Keeping the rules in mind, the teacher must get him involved in idealized, smoothed-out variations of the major fields of inquiry and knowledge. He must awaken the youth's awareness of hidden relations, and have him attend to unsuspected possibilities of combination and dissection.

All this adds up to the teacher knowing where the joints are, the places where the distinct is in fact united and where the whole is properly dismembered. Those joints are lost when a subject is divided to accord with the demands of a textbook, a calendar, or class periods, for then it is divided without regard to its structure and rationale—hardly a way to help students to become rational. Those joints are also lost when the idealization of a subject is confused with the simplification of it.

What is now taught in the schools for youths is in good part the product of an accidental accretion and modification of a curriculum going back to the Middle Ages. But a school should be the last place where things are done merely because they had been done before. Of all places, it should have its distinctions and connections grounded on justifying principles. Areas of difficulty, ignorance, and doubt should be remarked; the way these are related to the more familiar and intelligible areas should always be in focus. Were the secondary school organized by fully educated men, men who know what the final goal of man is and the stage to which a tween-ager can attain, it would undoubtedly have marked defects, but they would be other than those now evident, and they would presumably be eliminated by continuing the very process by which good results had already been achieved.

A youth is to be taught specific things, but in such a way that he will eventually understand his subjects in highly general terms. This is hard work that leaves no time for him to be taught driving or swimming during school hours. It is good for the youth to know how to drive or swim; the knowledge may save his life or the lives of others. But these should not be practiced in the secondary school. When then? Where? Is there any better place and time than in vocational schools operating after the formal school hours have ended? Society today often makes provision for the teaching of special creeds and the practices of particular religions, at other than regular school hours;

this would seem to be the suitable time when swimming and driving and similar useful skills, helpful in the preservation of life, can be profitably taught.

11]

The youth is to be taught special things. This is not the same thing as to say that he is to be presented with detached problems, or confronted only with subjects that are governed by methods easily mastered. He ought to be taught to see mathematics, science, history, and art as serious, full-bodied subjects, though he will not succeed in doing more than sense their distinctive lilt and characteristic objects, and will only begin the mastery of virtues which make further knowledge and discovery possible.

The youth should learn how to carry out a systematic train of reasoning. No one has found a better way for him to learn this than by his studying mathematics. Unfortunately, there is little agreement among mathematicians as to just how the subject is to be defined. But if we stand outside the different factions it becomes apparent, I think, that mathematics derives and describes the relations that hold between definite and constant possibilities.

The first counters used in mathematics were created in the course of a development of measurements, as the very term "geo-metry" makes evident. But it soon moved far beyond this humble practical beginning to deal with ideas and demonstrations for most of which there seems to be little or no practical use. Well-taught in mathematics, a student will never again suppose that the world of every day contains all that is, all that is interesting, or all that he ought to know. Most important, he will have learned to draw sound inferences and to use abstract, general terms with some skill.

Mathematicians complain that mathematics is taught badly in the secondary schools. They say that the teachers are incompetent, their knowledge outdated, and their teaching not in accord with the spirit of genuine mathematical thinking. They are met with the protest that it is wrong to treat students as though they were going to be professional mathematicians. The students, it is said, should instead be pointed toward the society and the world in which they will live their adult lives; the professional methods, analyses, concepts, and technical developments have nothing to do with the students' present or eventual interests and vocations.

We face here two parts of a single position. Both sides tacitly suppose that the students are to be prepared for later life, the one assuming that this is the intellectual world of the profession, the other assuming that this is the society as the adult now knows it. Both forget that the student is here and now. To teach him mathematics we need not acquaint him with what the profession endorses, nor with what the world of business or engineering requires. It is the task of the secondary school to help him become acquainted with a realm peopled by interrelated, highly general possibilities, more permanent and purer than anything he can encounter in daily life. He will then have achieved a distance from the mass of details which characterize his familiar world, and he will have sensed something of the rationale that connects all things because it embodies an eternal, rational order.

The tween-ager should also learn how to analyze and observe, to be careful and exacting. The justification for our teaching him science is that this offers the best means by which these results can be obtained. But no tween-ager can learn a science, if by science we mean the disciplined inquiry now pursued by creative scientists. Such science employs methods and techniques which take years and years to master. This is perhaps the reason why most secondary school teaching of science is little more than a presentation, usually in a highly dogmatic form, of the hypotheses and conclusions accepted by contemporary scientists. But these are of little value to the student, then or later; and most of them, in any case, can be readily found in dictionaries and encyclopedias and need not be stored in students' minds. Almost all are food for machines, not thoughts for the young.

We have much to answer for if we continue to make students accept the tentative positions of modern scientific thought as though they expressed fixed truths about the nature of things. Science, like mathematics, is worthy of being taught to the tween-ager because it takes him beyond the world of the commonplace, the transient, and the unruly, to the steady principles and laws that govern every part of the cosmos. If correctly taught it helps him learn how to engage in controlled inquiry, under well-defined circumstances, honestly and carefully. He will then come to know empirical and testable truths which have an import that transcends the here and now.

There are many sciences. No one has time enough to teach them all; no one has time enough to learn them all. Which should be selected for teaching in the secondary schools? Most teachers would say "physics." There is good reason for the choice; physics has a glorious history of brilliant predictions. And there are many who are engaged in sciences other than physics who speak as though their disciplines dealt with nothing more than compounds of the elements and laws studied in physics. I think they are mistaken. But whether they are or not, physics is not the most suitable science to be taught to the tween-ager.

It is the very virtues of physics that make it have comparatively less value to the youth than other sciences, for no youth is in a position to grasp the import of a discipline which ranges from the cosmic at one end to the submicroscopic at the other. Chemistry, because more terrestrial, is more within the youth's power, both conceptually and experimentally. However, it lacks immediacy; it does not readily appeal to the student's sense of wonder, particularly when, in its modern form, it relies so much on physical analyses and discoveries. More in consonance with the youth's appetites, abilities, and tastes are geography and biology, with the latter preferred since it is more in accord with the temper of the other sciences.

A study of biology allows the student not only to learn something of the essence of a science, but also to understand something of himself in relation to the other inhabitants of our earth. But far too many biology teachers assume without question that their subject is occupied only with complex physical and chemical compounds. Were they right, there would be little reason for teaching biology to the youth; the more basic physics and chemistry would give them their biology in a purer and broader form. But biology also includes ecology, the study of the interinvolvement of living organisms. At present ecology has a large descriptive component, and is overly oriented toward problems of conservation and pollution. But there is no reason why it should not be taught in such a way as to communicate the spirit of the great naturalists. Darwin was one of them. I would have his interests recovered.

Observation has techniques and methods which a youth can learn more readily than he can the techniques and methods of experimentation. It is doubtful whether he can profit much from clumsy attempts at dissection. How much better it would be to have him get some sense of the wonder of life and the variety of its forms. He should be readied to note the ways of birds and fish, and even of his own dog or cat; he has much to learn from visits to zoos and from field trips.

History primarily and politics secondarily are subjects for the secondary school because they teach students how to organize vital material along temporal and humanly important lines. This fact is missed if we take history to be a simple ordering of events or a process of dating past occurrences. History is no sequence of tales spun out over remote periods; for the historian it is a living inquiry which, starting with present evidences, seeks to discover the past explanatory causes of what those evidences reveal. His narration of the sequence of events which led from the causes to what they explain is guided by the idea of the relevant and important—very difficult ideas to focus on. This is evidently not the history that is or should be taught to the youth.

No youth knows how to collect evidence, nor how to move back into the past for the source of it. And if he could arrive at that past, he would not know how to move forward again to the present with which he began. Could he make that move, he would not know how to narrate what had happened, or show how it conditions what follows. But what a youth can do is to so read an historic narrative that he partakes vicariously in the great crises, events, and achievements of man. If as a consequence he comes to see the present world to be in good part the product of the past, he will find himself enriched, enlightened, and perhaps stimulated to prepare to assume an historic role eventually.

It is sad to think of how much history teaching in the primary and secondary schools is little more than a series of remarks on how quaint other people's ideas, customs, and practices are. Instead of teaching we then promote provincialism. When tween-agers, near certain holidays, are asked to dress up as Pilgrims, Indians, or Founding Fathers, they are not taught history but instead are encouraged to exhibit their inability to act. What is needed is a narrating that promotes the tween-ager's acceptance of what was great in the tradition in which he is to share.

Much history is political in orientation; much politics is historically conditioned. But the two disciplines have different interests and roles. History has no structure which can be read out in advance; it acquires one when and as it moves along. Politics instead presupposes a structure, or rather a plurality of structures governing organizations whose ultimate warrant is their capacity to sustain and promote the commonweal. Within those organizations and subject to those structures, men interact with one another and with those who have assumed the position of leaders and controls. But students are rarely taught about real politics, even in those classes devoted exclusively to the subject. Instead they are lulled by tales about a harmonious union of dedicated men and efficient agencies, all selflessly devoted to the spread of sunshine and the preservation of the nation's glory. Since little or nothing is said about the inexorable power struggle, about the interplay of economic forces and political ambitions, or about the pettiness and limited vision of those who are in control, the student is offered fiction and myth in place of fact. These will be swept away at his first contact with bureaucracy and timeservers.

Though we have no hesitation about telling a child about wicked and foolish kings, we seem to think that the youth must hear only good of those who are in authority. He ought not to be turned into a crude cynic, but this is not the same thing as to say that we must not allow him to know any of the realities of politics. Respect for the state and its attempt to enforce law and order can be encouraged without resorting to falsehoods or evasions.

The youth need not be taught the nature of the state as it is in fact. It would be better indeed to tell him what the state should ideally be. To learn about the ideal is to learn to see beyond the petty acts that make up the ordinary political day. The ideal should be exhibited as that which not only lies beyond the horizon of the state in fact, but as that which ought to guide it. If instead it is presented as fact, truth will be submerged in sentiment and the ground will be laid for disaffection and resentment.

No young person ever gets more than a glimpse of the nature of the ideal state. But this may prove enough to give him some understanding of what is and what can be, what might have been and what ought to be. Then and later he will be more alert to what must be done if men are to live together in peace and prosperity.

Art too belongs in the youth's curriculum. By its means he can improve his sight and insight, and give play to his creative abilities and powers of expression. But which of the many arts should he be taught? Architecture is too complex. Painting and sculpture are hard to free from daily images and familiar scenes. Music, acting, and dancing have little communicable content, little which can be readily articulated, reexamined, or restructured. But literature seems most suitable. This is not because it makes use of language. The language of story and poetry are just as alien to the language of daily prose as painted colors and shapes are to those of nature. If anything, an acquaintance with the daily prose of a language offers an obstacle to the proper use of it in an art. Poetry and stories are written and read as works of art only when their words and sentences are used in ways that are distinct from those characteristic of daily discourse.

The child becomes part of a wider world through the medium of a story. For the youth to become aware of a world subtending the familiar he must become acquainted with literature, i.e., with poetry, stories, and plays which have artistic merit. He will then achieve an insight into a root reality which is at times tragic and at times comic, but always dynamic and pertinent, dark and omnipresent. Through literature he will learn what it is to be in a world he never made, but of which he must take account, bodily, mentally, and emotionally.

Pursued in an atmosphere of friendly criticism provided by a knowledgeable teacher, the different studies bring the youth to the edge of seeing what is ideal, i.e., what is not yet fully realized in this world. Through those studies some information will be conveyed, some acquaintance with different methods, instruments, and agencies will inevitably be achieved. But the youth will not have been taught properly if he has not been helped to forge his character.

By the time the youth is on the verge of entering the

world of men, he should have built up steady habits of honesty, reflection, and reasonableness. He should be able to work despite obstacles, and to be willing and ready to teach himself along the lines already laid out. Only then will he be prepared to move into the second half of the decade that precedes the time when he can function as a mature man. Only then will he have moved beyond the point where he primarily seeks a place for himself in a world which carries its past within itself, to the point where he is attentive to the values that govern all enterprises and are embodied in whatever he confronts.

3

On the Verge of Manhood

THE EDUCATED, ARISTOCRATIC CLASS has known for centuries—and we now accept the fact without question—that young men, not only youths, need to be formally educated. To this we today have added a truth which should have been accepted even before the other: all men have a right to obtain whatever education they can profit from. It is our combination of these truths that is behind the unusual, American practice of encouraging most young men, of around eighteen to twenty-two, to go to college.

Some colleges are little more than preparatory schools for medicine, law, and other technical disciplines. They are the regrettable products of a pressure exerted by graduate and professional schools. The students in those colleges are treated as children were once dealt with in the primary school, as essentially promissory beings to be prepared but not to be then and there fulfilled. But college students have distinctive rights and problems. They deserve to be given appropriate work and to be taught subjects appropriate to their powers and their promise.

The properly educated youth has acquired a character, a stabilized set of virtues and powers enabling him to exercise a considerable measure of self-control. His will can direct not only his body but his mind and often his emotions as well. Well-established rules, approved categories, classifications, and principles have been mastered by him, and as a consequence he has become part of a tradition punctuated by great, inspiring men and events. By engaging in activities which require the skilled use of distinctive powers, he has learned how to judge reasonably and often rationally. Having tested himself again and again against other youths as well as against the time, the space, the laws, and the forces of existence, he is now able to use the techniques which are prerequisites for any steady effective involvement in man's major enterprises. He is now ready to live as a young man. But he still needs to be educated in college.

Where the youth is taught how to maintain himself in a public world, the young man must be taught how to understand and use that world in the most effective ways known to civilized man. While living privately over against the rest of the world, he must learn to live on a footing with it. Since he runs the risk of becoming self-centered, we must instead teach him how to become a center, making judgments of more than momentary import.

Accepting their teachers as qualified judges, students can learn how to treat the past as a storehouse of knowledge and experience, and gradually adopt that set of ideal values which mark the civilized man. Ideally their teacher is a master of a basic enterprise. Only he can make the students concern themselves with matters whose conquest require the students' full attention and energy.

College is the time for the student to learn what subjects ideally are, while engaged in them in limited, rather blundering, quite mundane ways. The desired product of the college is a man who looks at the world with generosity and thoughtfulness, alert to its major nuances, and actively or vicariously sharing in all the dimensions of human achievement.

2]

The ordinary adult is a practical man. At his best
he is a craftsman in the field of effective living. But
even then he is not all a man should be. Having sacrificed
much in order to make a delimited portion of the world
more or less his home, instead of being a man of the world
he is a part only of a part of it. Every man must occupy a
similar, limited area. But he will not have fully realized his
potentiality for being a man unless at the same time he is
aware of values he himself does not sustain or pursue, but
which are as basic as those which he cherishes. While
limited and involved in special tasks, he has to learn how to
be part of the richer world.

College is where a student should begin to learn the art
of living in a multifaceted, civilized world, set in a vast,
indifferent space, with a long, impersonal, temporal span.
The apprenticeship will be tedious and without much of a
future if the student is not exposed to the major fields of
human endeavor in their full muscularity. Only if he is so
exposed will he be able to find the area in which he can
later spend most of his energies, doing most justice to his
talents and interests. Denied this opportunity, he will be
unable to appreciate the fact that there are many choices of
equal merit, and that he is to make use of what other men
produce while he contributes to what they themselves can
use in their own ways.

If education is to be the art of readying a man to
become complete, it must concern itself with the attainment of attitudes which make completion most likely.
These attitudes are prepared for in the period of youth. It
was then that industry, self-confidence, modesty, and charity should have been ingrained. In college, these attitudes
are to be sharpened, forced to face hard cases, and supple-

mented in various ways. They are to be backed by skills (by means of which the student will eventually be able to work without guidance) as well as by a mastery of instruments for communication and an effective struggle with nature. And resources should be provided in the form of records of great works and thoughts that make up the body of the tradition out of which we all have grown, of which we all make use, and to which, we trust, all of us will eventually contribute.

Students ought to learn what man has ventured and what man has achieved. But to keep students turned to the past alone is to support the supposition that only the dead have a right to be known as creative men. Students should participate in the grand movement of civilization, not only by enjoying its fruits, but by getting ready to be vital parts themselves of the new epoch about to begin. Not all will be interested in doing this; few will produce anything of magnitude. But most can be helped through education to make some use of their creative powers. And everyone can learn to understand what he is, and what he can do. All can at least be prepared to support others in their creative endeavors, and should be prepared to cherish and enjoy what these produce.

The hope of education is that what was begun in college will be carried out in later life by a more mature, better disciplined, more knowledgeable, independent, creative man. This is not a prospect which has caught the imagination of many college administrators, educational theorists, or teachers. They put together the curriculum and arrange the calendar, they regulate and define the obligations and rights of student and teacher on no discernible principle. Almost unconsciously, and surely persistently, most educators bind themselves and others to a half-forgotten, largely irrelevant practice, unwarranted in fact or in theory, and serving as little more than an agency for protecting vested interests and power. In no other place except college are subjects required and work assigned so arbitrarily. Nowhere else do we find so little evidence of a reasoned or a rational plan. The kind of thinking and programing that passes for curriculum study, the most tolerant of professors would find unacceptable in his own classroom. Why he tolerates them in his colleagues and exhibits it himself is one of the mysteries of higher education.

3]

There are now available in print a number of reputable discussions about the elementary school and what it should do. We are beginning to make some sense of the secondary school. But college in theory and practice is chaos, a miscellany whose content tells us where academic politics is most successful. It is time to try to understand what a college ought to be.

College students need to be made alert to the values which are central to a civilized life and to the truths and goods that ennoble the passage of time. Division of the curriculum into subjects should increase students' insight and knowledge. If those subjects enable teachers to exhibit in their persons the glory of a manly and honest struggle with major truths and serious problems, we have reason enough to divide the curriculum. If a particular division is not produced in order to assure these results, we can defend it only on the grounds that it matches the major divisions of being or practice, or that any other division is no better and might be worse. But even this feeble thesis has never been clearly stated and defended.

Ideally a college recognizes that all self-critical, disciplined inquiry deserves its support and encouragement. Since it is the college's function to provide for the communication and achievement of great truths, it takes all root knowledge to be within its province. If we wish—and in some sense we must—to have distinct subjects in a college, only those should be accepted which preserve pivotal insights and knowledge regarding man, civilization, and the cosmos, and then only so far as the subjects use and make available methods of research and communication which have proved to be successful over the course of the teacher's life or that of a community of scholars.

It is possible to proceed without disaster for considerable time even when the determination of what is and is not to be taught is decided by administrative whim, the interests of scholars, the demands of the day, and the need for some order. But risk there surely is. Poorly grounded methods usually fail us in crucial places. They will not help us decide whether or not some of the subjects which are taught in some colleges—pedagogy, public speaking, local government—are to be allowed to remain. Without an understanding of what it is that the student ought to learn, we will not be able to evaluate properly the claims now being made on behalf of new subjects such as business administration, the study of great debates, the history of exploration, space travel, and the ethics of business. To deal with such issues in something like the spirit in which one conducts a college class or a scientific inquiry, recourse must be had to a more systematic procedure.

A college subject seeks, promotes, supports and communicates the essential features of the cosmos, civilization and man. Making a maximum use of man's power to know and learn it attempts to provide an understanding and explanation of whatever there be. This means that it must be governed by a vision of the whole of things and of knowledge. If it failed to express and sustain such a vision, it would be but a fragment of an inquiry, having no necessary importance in a larger context, and no necessary connection with any other. If a college were to teach such subjects it would more likely than not have no time left for anything else. What could be more desirable? At one stroke it would be doing what it ought, and freeing itself from the multiple irrelevancies which now so occupy it.

A vision of the whole of things and of knowledge as a

rule is not explicitly acknowledged, even by those subjects which exhibit and promote it. There is no harm in this. But it is one thing to have no insight at all into the way in which all things and all knowledges are interrelated, and another not to have this insight to the fore.

The departmentalization of subjects, the competition among intellectuals for prestige and power, the influence of professional associations, and perhaps even the need to make use of special habits, techniques, and instruments have in recent years tempted scholars to abandon an interest in far-ranging subjects and to replace them by limited specialties. As a consequence they have found that their primary loyalty was not to their colleagues in other fields, or to their institutions and the students there, but to fellow-specialists in other places. One sad side effect of this shift has been a turning away from the humanistic teaching of undergraduates to research abetted by subordinates and federal funds, with the consequence that colleges and universities have begun to take on the appearance of research institutes, with a regrettable loss of interest in teaching, and without any visible gain in the quality or quantity of knowledge.

A specialist soon gets himself into the paradoxical position of subjecting his own studies to the most careful and critical of tests, while accepting, naïvely and blindly, whatever the other specialists tell him they have discovered or have agreed upon. How odd it is to be dubious about what one knows best, and to be receptive toward all else. Why should one refuse to be firm with regard to anything within the area of his own competence and study, while remaining most receptive to what is reported by those who have specialized elsewhere? The paradox cannot be avoided unless one has some overall view.

Different subjects achieve results of different degrees of value. Not all are on a level; they do not all cohere with one another. If there were nothing but a plurality of completely independent disciplines, one could have no assurance that they would ever yield a single body of knowledge. And, since the different disciplines would not necessarily have the same criteria of excellence, truth, or precision, there would be no way of determining, when a selection had to be made from them, which was to be preferred. If we are to know what the various subjects presuppose, if only in an unreflecting and blurred way, we will have to make room for a discipline which takes as its major concern the mastery of what the others acknowledge, though only implicitly.

4]

    A college is a unity from every position; every subject in it, following its own bent, should exhibit and sustain a common vision. Each should seek certifiable truths of importance for men everywhere, today and tomorrow. Each in specialized ways should manifest and promote a grasp of the whole of things and of knowledge, to give us a mosaic of comprehensive visions in place of a chaos of limited specialties.

Each subject in the ideal college offers a highly developed form of man's perpetual quest for understanding what it is to be and to know. This statement rests on two important claims. It supposes that what ordinary men say and do is not altogether satisfactory; it also supposes that college work differs in degree and not in kind from that in which ordinary men engage. Were men in their daily rounds capable of adequately knowing all there is or ought to be known, there would be little stimulus and less warrant for the pursuit of higher learning; were men in their daily rounds different in type from the scholar, it would be hard to see how one could ever communicate with or become the other. The powers which the scholar develops and exploits are latent in the ordinary man. They become explicit only under the force of self-discipline, persistence, and dedication, the marks of the true scholar.

When we say anything in daily life, we make use of a minimal body of acquired knowledge and maintain, at least implicitly, that we are men like others, exercising a typical degree of competence in observation and language. In effect we are then claiming to be qualified to speak for all, precisely because we make use of powers present in all. The scholar goes further than the ordinary man to say what anyone in principle could, but what most now cannot and will not be likely to say because they do not use and develop the necessary relevant interests and energies. This is not to deny that there are differences in talent and virtue, in degrees of intelligence, perceptiveness, and insight; it is to deny that mankind falls into multiple species, with some qualified in principle to do what others in principle could not possibly do.

Those men alone are qualified to teach in a college who make the most effective use of capacities to inquire, criticize, communicate, and create that are present in all. Such qualified men are representatives of the rest, representatively using the power that all men possess, but which most do not use except occasionally and in a minor way. The ideal teacher pushes back the borders of what is already known, and tries to add significantly to what can be rationally defended and accepted by honest men. He tries to awaken the will to inquiry and to the acceptance of what is true, in part by offering himself and his work as a model. When most successful, he frees students from complete immersion in purely local and individual concerns, making them effective and putting them on the road to being knowledgeable and wise.

Just as the college is the universe caught within the frame of conscientious reflection, so each subject is the college in miniature, caught within the frame of some distinctive mode of inquiry. Each subject offers itself as a source and explanation of the rest; each provides a basic approach to every other's subject matter. Chemistry, in principle, offers an account of thought and action, of crime and illness, of man and nature, of the practice and intent of art, philosophy, and theology. And what is true of chemistry is true of the other genuine college subjects. Were this not the case, the world of knowledge and being would be divided into islands, each with its own topography, acquaintance with which would not help one elsewhere. It would, in the derogatory sense that artists have made popular, be just an "academic" subject.

Each subject has its own rationale. An approach to one from the perspective of some other is therefore bound to do less than full justice to its intent and content. This is the truth that all reductionists overlook, materialists as well as idealists, physicalists as well as existentialists. These men sometimes offer perspectives from which they can embrace the whole gamut of being and knowledge, and grasp the nature of other disciplines. But then they forget that their perspectives are limited; inevitably they distort the intent and the content of the rest. Even more regrettably, they tend to dismiss other approaches as useless or unintelligible, seemingly unaware that the others can and do take the same attitude toward them.

Sociology encompasses physics as surely as physics does sociology. But neither does justice to what the other in fact is in its own terms. Neither replaces the other. No approach completely masters the world as it is grasped from other positions. Each subject has its own particular bias and must be supplemented by others. The teaching of the physical and social sciences, art, theology, history, and the classics can be justified because of their universality, a universality which is lacking to agriculture, dentistry, and public speaking. If these three are to be included in a college curriculum, they must be shown to be subdivisions of the others, somewhat as anatomy and obstetrics are of medicine, and torts and contracts are of law.

It is of course possible to use any subject whatsoever as an epitomization of whatever there be, if sufficient interpretation is imposed on its included items, or if its principles are made sufficiently flexible. Even dentistry can be supposed to be a worthy college subject, since it can be viewed as offering a model for the efficient use of basic tools, or as providing the ground for all endeavors, in view of the fact that the child's life begins with a concentration on its oral needs. But no matter how we twist and turn we cannot show that dentistry is grounded in a vision of the whole of things and knowledge. It does not offer a primary way in which we can come to understand and adjust ourselves to what is real. Nor is it entailed by some comprehensive understanding and explanation of the nature of civilization, man, or the cosmos.

5]

It is desirable for the student to come to know the main branches of knowledge, the basic dimensions of reality, the great achievements of the past, and the components of civilization. One way to do this is to have him take comprehensive courses. Almost every college has had its little adventure with one or more of these. Surveys, orientation programs, and general educational plans are tried out almost everywhere and every year. There are few who would claim that any of them has proved to be signally successful. The failure has been due in part to the fact that leading teachers could not be persuaded to teach them, in part to the fact that the courses dealt with more than most teachers know or most students can assimilate, and in part to the fact that the material was offered in the shape of large generalities, serving primarily only to introduce the student to what were supposed to be the serious specialties taught in the higher level courses. I do not think that these difficulties are insuperable. In any case the courses could be improved. A more careful consideration of what ought to be covered, a better prepared, more mature teaching staff, and a more precise and vigorous treatment of pivotal ideas and events would make the surveys more valuable than they now are.

A good case can be made out for surveys which deal

with nature, man, and society, provided that the courses are carefully planned and well-taught by seasoned men. Offered at the very beginning of the college career they will provide a needed systematic introduction to the nature of living and nonliving things and to the essence of great discoveries, inventions, thoughts, and creative works. Ideally, they will make the student alert to both the humanistic and the exact branches of knowledge, to subhuman realities as well as to man as he exists over space and time. Such surveys could be usefully followed by specialties in which what had been dealt with in a broad way and for a short time would be treated with greater precision and in more detail. Together the various specialties would thoroughly articulate what had been covered before. The specialties would then all contribute to a richer, single totality where they supported one another. That totality could then be made the topic of a final integrated course where nature, man, and society were dealt with once more, but as illumined by the spirit and content of the different specialties.

Were this suggestion followed, the student at the beginning and end of his college career would come to know the world of which he now is and will be a part. But is it possible to organize such courses without some understanding of the basic divisions of knowledge that the nature of the world supports? To know what subjects are to be taught in college it is necessary to know what reality is and where its primary joints are. This means we must engage in philosophic reflection. This is the only known process by which one can hope to make any totality of particulars intelligible and rational. It is not easy to carry through, persistently and clearly. We run a risk of ending with only surmises and abstractions. But the price is not too high if it is men we are planning to make.

6]

The hope of civilized mankind is that our young will soon become vital parts of civilization. This is not the same thing as their becoming a part of a world. Civilization is a totality of values, but a world is only a totality of facts. We fit into a world by knowing and adjusting ourselves to what occurs, but we can arrive at civilization only if we attend to realities beyond the horizon of daily life.

A student should be taught, not the nature of a world, but the realities on which the world rests and which it partly obscures. We must help him become nonempirical, for only the nonempirically minded is ever at home with what is finally real. Only he will know what explains, clarifies, and sustains what occurs in fact. College is the time and place to teach useless subjects. Only useless subjects? Yes, only useless subjects, even if one wanted—indeed, precisely if one wants—to give the student a "practical" education. We know and adjust best to the world of facts when we know what it presupposes.

The realities which transcend the world can be known in four ways: in their purity; as affecting the world; as affecting man; and as governing, theoretically and practically, man in his interplay with whatever there be. And all of us know them more or less in these four ways. When we think rigorously and when we reflect on the principles which govern our lives or thoughts, we make some use of truths that express what is real in its purity. When we occupy ourselves with art, sociology, psychology, and related fields, we instead attend to the way in which ultimate realities affect the world and man. Our interest in history, economics, and politics finally reflect the realities which structure man's interplay with man and other things.

History, etc. are too often treated as though they dealt only with factual material, minor hypotheses, and inductive summaries. But they have this dismal shape only when their results are disconnected from the process of their attainment, when facts are divorced from principles, and appearances are held apart from the realities which ground them. But even those who understand their subjects in the light of principles rooted in what lies beyond the world of facts tend to deny that they know anything about any beings that lie beyond. They grant that the principles govern the subjects, but they think that the principles can exist nowhere else but in those subjects. This is certainly a plausible stand to take with respect to most disciplines. But it will not do for philosophy, or logic, or mathematics. Let us see why.

4

The College Curriculum

THE COLLEGE STUDENT is on the verge of manhood. To take him most effectively where he ought to go, we must show him how to approach all questions from the position of sound principles and final truths. This means we must acquaint him with disciplines which range wide and dig deep.

We need a sound base if we are to construct a college curriculum in a rational manner. Philosophy, logic, and mathematics provide that base; they attend to what is presupposed by all disciplines (including themselves). Unfortunately there are no established characterizations of any of them. In such a situation it seems wise to offer one's own account of them, even though the result will almost inevitably have a regrettable dogmatic tonality. But I offer the following remarks on the main features of the basic disciplines to be taught in a college only as suggestions regarding the content and warrant of higher education.

2]

Philosophy is a self-critical and yet radically sympathetic adventure seeking to determine those categories which are exemplified by everything, the realities which ground all else, and the principles which all knowing illustrates. At once analytic and creative, it unites proof and imagination to present a scheme enabling one to understand what man is, what he can do and has done, and the nature of the universe in which he lives.

Philosophy is no synthesis of other subjects. Nor does it build on their results. To master it we need not first master other disciplines. Were it a synthesis or did it depend on a prior mastery of other subjects, philosophy would have to know the others. This would require it to wait for the time when these others were sufficiently complete and compatible to make possible their clarification and harmonization. But until then would they not be without guidance? Who would examine and evaluate their grounds today? Would not their presuppositions remain unexamined; would not their truths be isolated, unrelated to one another? These questions mark the beginning of a philosophic inquiry.

All subjects need the supplementation and neutrality which philosophy provides. It is tempting to infer from this observation that philosophy is superior to the others, or that it is the source or guaranty of their truths. The temptation must be resisted. Each of the basic disciplines has its own problems; each follows distinctive methods to arrive at distinctive goals; each has its own store of truths which it certifies in its own way.

The subjects which deserve to be taught in a college have three distinctive marks. They embody a common purpose, they exploit powers others allow to remain latent or which they use improperly, and they offer a special perspective on other fields and disciplines. Philosophy is no exception.

Like other basic subjects, philosophy is sustained by a vision of the whole of things. Like them, it allows this vision to quicken and to guide it. But unlike other disciplines philosophy makes its basic vision into a topic of investigation. Though this is the express concern only of certain courses in philosophy, it would be hard to retain as a course in philosophy one which did not constantly examine that vision both sympathetically and critically. All courses in philosophy provide a viable root knowledge of what is—which all men in a sense already know—and of what should govern or guide their more important activities.

Philosophy can be understood and even pursued without special training; it can, as no other subject does or can, talk to and for all subjects about the man, the society, and the cosmos they all presuppose. Yet it is not easy to become a philosopher. Normally it takes a lifetime before one is broad-ranged enough, independently-minded enough, self-critical enough to think through the problems that have confronted reflective men across the ages. No one who has been indifferent to the achievements of the great philosophers of the past, who is unaware of their errors and discoveries, can hope to make much progress in philosophy. It is an old man's subject best taught by one near the end of his career—though those younger may be more lively, keener, more knowledgeable, and influential.

Philosophy is to be taught to the young for somewhat the same reason that a survey course, though desirable at the end of a college career, is also to be taught at the beginning—because it gives the young man an opportunity to grasp the range and basic connections of all that he is to know. But where a survey course deals with past achievements, the discoveries of laws and patterns, and the essentials of the various disciplines, philosophy takes account only of the presuppositions, categories, and problems which everything illustrates.

Philosophy would be a mere specialty alongside others, which they might blindly accept or (as is usually the case) ignore, did its account not offer a ground for what the rest affirm, and were its methods and tests not open to any intelligent man's examination. What it says can be tested by seeing whether or not it clarifies what other disciplines claim and point toward, by seeing if it shows how they and their achievements can be part of one body of being and knowledge, and by seeing whether or not it does justice to what the various specialists do and know outside their academic pursuits. The answers will at no time assume the shape of simple affirmations or denials. A philosopher sometimes points to realms unsuspected by the specialists, and which they can acknowledge only by altering concept, procedure, or direction. Specialized work in turn sometimes opens up areas beyond the surmise of the most speculative of men, and which they can acknowledge only by restructuring their entire enterprise.

Most students and administrators know philosophy primarily as one of the fields of higher learning which make use of important human powers. In this role it asks such questions as: What is right? What is true? What ought to be? What is real? These questions are usually expressly dealt with in so-called systematic courses. But the history of philosophy is also a part of philosophy. Were it not concerned with basic problems and their solution, it would be at best only a parade of discarded and often quaint conceits. But it is hard to understand how one can say this without forgetting that some of the classical philosophers were men of genius, who made many observations still revelant to what we now know, do, and are. A systematic study completely cut off from the history of philosophy would foolishly ignore the wisdom of the past and the lessons that had been taught by illustrious predecessors.

Recently a new type of course has been making room for itself in many colleges. It has an old name, and its ideals are something like those that prevailed in late scholasticism. I refer to modern logic. Too often its practitioners resolutely put aside an examination of their preconceptions, and refuse to discuss the foundations or import of their subject. Exactitude need not preclude adventure. Were logicians more daring, they would provide more illumination than they now do, of whatever there is and is to be known. Instead they concentrate on the disciplining and training of young men in a highly technical set of operations, and sometimes even in the use of purely mechanical devices. Logic is not so interesting, so flexible, or so creative as mathematics, nor so useful as laboratory training in the sciences or workshop practice in the arts. Were we courageous and clearheaded enough, modern logic would be relegated to the secondary school, where it would be taught as an established technique, and to the graduate school, where it would be taught as an enterprise engaged in the discovery or investigation of untried or new techniques.

Modern logic is an exciting field; its problems and techniques are important, and might conceivably help us deal effectively and decisively with neglected areas of thought, and perhaps even with some of the problems which have defied solution over the ages. But if it is not pursued in a philosophic spirit, it cannot rightly be termed a philosophic subject, deserving a place in a college curriculum. To achieve such a place it must become more self-critical than it now is. If it does not offer a distinctive perspective on reality and knowledge, logic does not merit a place in the humanities, the sciences, or the arts.

One branch of philosophy is occupied with offering a neutral, rationally sustained account of ultimate reality. There are not many philosophers who are qualified to engage in it. But a number of them could together offer what no one might be able to do separately. Will they not then form a school? Not necessarily. The likelihood indeed is the opposite. Schools tend to be doctrinaire, refusing to subject themselves to self-examination, and acknowledging no other approach. This is precisely what a group of men who are working properly together will not do. From different positions they will make evident a multifaceted universe, grounding a plurality of equally respectable perspectives.

If one could recover an interest in the entire range of philosophic inquiry by means of a department, the work of philosophy could be covered in a set of courses taught by different men. But whether the whole of philosophy is presented by an individual or a group, the outcome of philosophic reflection, and something of its spirit, can be known and used in every philosophic course, and, hopefully through these, in every part of the college. Ideally, philosophers not only teach but are practicing philosophers as well.

It is philosophy's function to provide a neutral, all-encompassing account of things and of knowledge. This no other subject does. But in turn, philosophy cannot do what they can. It neither predicts nor helps resolve questions of particular matters of fact, and in addition is inescapably abstract, achieving its neutrality by cutting itself off from concrete investigations. But because it is neutral and abstract, it is able to explain what being and knowledge are, can provide a justification for its own existence and activity, can expose the bases for other enterprises and can make evident that common experience out of which they all issue.

Philosophy affirms that other subjects presuppose much that they do not examine or ever justify. With equal justice they affirm that philosophy is at once too general and too critical, controlling no facts, making no empirical discoveries. Both are right. But both are mistaken if they then suppose that they have exposed a weakness in the other. Each has legitimate tasks and distinctive criteria, calling for a union of insight and courage, discipline and sensitivity, knowledge and creativity. Only together can they do justice to man's need to be and to know. They need one another. Were they wise enough, philosophers and nonphilosophers would seek one another out for what would complete what each alone achieves.

At its best, a philosophic account of the universe of knowledge and being can guide and ground every other activity. To get to this position philosophy must carry out processes of analysis, speculation, and criticism to their ultimate limits. It will then achieve a perspective in terms of which every enterprise can be explained and understood.

Philosophy both encompasses and is correlative to all other subjects — most effectively if others accept it for what it is. If they will both follow and supplement it, they will become more aware of what they are, what they are doing, what they assume, what is outside their reach, and what it is that each, in its own way, and all of them together are trying to know.

The philosopher's role in the college is the role he also has outside. This is nothing more or less than to be a philosopher for himself and for others. The wise administrator will seek out the true philosopher to learn what can be known from one whose range is wide, whose sympathies are deep, and whose criticisms are steady and fair. He whom the philosopher really teaches is fortunate indeed. Though he will have learned few facts and truths, he will have had his vision widened and thereby become aware of what is genuinely worth knowing.

3]

What is usually taught the college student in the name of mathematics is not this subject but at residue of it. Rarely is he introduced to the living adventure of mathematical thinking. Instead he is given formulae and shown techniques that have been discovered by men of genius and which are now applied in science or engineering. The subject he is then taught has no more place in college than a language drill; it is no more justified than is the teaching of driving or swimming in high school.

Mathematics unites what most think must be forever opposed: it links possibilities by means of necessities. Creatively precise, it explores a realm of possibilities of the highest generality, trying to make evident their necessary connections. Since everything whatsoever instances possibilities, mathematics is exemplified in everything. Though it says nothing directly about the world, since it says what is necessary, it inevitably tells what is true always. No matter how transient and contingent an occurrence is, there is a necessity within it linking the possibilities which the occurrence momentarily exemplifies.

Mathematicians use their minds. This has led some people to hold that mathematics has to do only with what is mentally created. But of what subject can this not be said? Presumably too there will *be* no minds, since on this view a mind would be created inside some other mind, and this inside another, and so on without end. The meaning of science, and the world that mathematics knows, are seriously jeopardized by this and other misconceptions.

Mathematicians use their minds to discover, not to uncover, what is necessarily possible. It takes great imagination, inventiveness, and insight on their part to arrive at the point where their thoughts accord with the way in which possibilities attract, repel, affiliate, and merge with one another. The study of mathematics should help one to minimize misunderstandings of the nature and reality of the possibilities that sometimes exist inside and always exist outside the borders of our daily world.

Mathematicians use signs. Sometimes they create new symbols and subject them to distinct types of rule in an endeavor to overcome some glaring asymmetries in formulae or system. It is therefore tempting to take mathematics to be only a language, arbitrary and artificial in nature, with rejectable rules that happen to be agreed upon. But then one would in effect deny that there are necessities in mathematics, referring to the unbreakable links between the possibilities that are symbolized by the mathematical signs.

Mathematicians sometimes publish. Since publishing requires a systematic presentation of what one knows, it is tempting to suppose that mathematics offers a systematic account of what the mathematician knows. But the systematization follows on a genuine process of mathematical thinking. This is much freer, much more creative, and much more episodic than the articles in the journals and the textbooks make evident.

Mathematics is a college subject. It should be within the competence of every college student. All deserve to know what pure possibilities are like; they will then know something of the structure of eternity and something about the rationality that lies at the root of every subject and every thing. All should therefore be taught to engage in mathematical thinking, with its interweaving of rigor and imagination, clarity and insight, ingenuity and submission to the facts.

4]

There is a history of art and a making of art. The first presupposes the second. But in many colleges the first is taught but the second is not. And in almost all the rest the first was taught long before the second was given a place in the curriculum.

Should artists teach the making of art? They are, after all, notoriously inarticulate and unacquainted with the well-established teaching methods. Still, it is only they who have gone through the process of creating works, and therefore are alone acquainted with what can be done, and the requirements which must be met if it is to be done. We misconstrue what teaching artists are doing if we look at them as though they were somewhat like the teachers of the humanities, for they are essentially coaches who do not convey information but offer advice and suggestions, and indicate where corrections, omissions, and additions would make an important difference. Their main concern is to try to get the student to free himself from traditional limitations and unnecessary restrictions. When the artists insist that the student master his medium and exercise his creative powers they are helping him make the best use of the only means by which beauty can be produced, and the dynamic space-time underlying our daily world made evident.

In recent years many colleges have made provision for the teaching of some arts. But rarely are the performing arts, particularly dancing, allowed a place in male-oriented colleges. Not many academic institutions have classes in photography, graphic design, architecture, the writing of poetry, novels and plays, or the production of movies. What is taught in most is musical appreciation, painting, and the writing or performing of music. But there is no reason, except historic accident, why these should be preferred to the others.

There are a number of plausible ways of describing and relating the arts, and it would be better to accept anyone of these ways rather than to follow the usual practice of haphazardly making room for this art and excluding that. I have found it desirable to distinguish between the spatial, temporal, and dynamic arts. Sculpture, architecture, and painting can then be said to be occupied with the creation of space; music, story, and poetry with the creation of time; and dancing and acting with the creation of vital processes of becoming, all in sensuous forms.

It is often said that music is the greatest of the arts. But there have been those who have given first place to poetry, painting, or drama instead. It seems wiser to assume that all the arts are on a footing until experience or sound theory teaches us otherwise. But whatever our decision we are up against the fact that no student can master all the arts. If he could, he would have no time for other subjects.

Rarely can more than one art be mastered by a student. Since students differ too much in aptitude, training, and interest to make it desirable for all to be involved in the same art, a proper curriculum will make it possible for different students to learn different arts. Each will then have an opportunity to choose from among a number of arts that one which is most suitable to his talents and temper.

Any one of the arts can help the student develop his powers of discrimination and judgment; any one of them can make evident the conventionality of daily life and practice, the joy of creation, the controlled expression of the emotions, and the texture, lilt, complexity, and roots of the world. We should teach all the basic arts in order to make it possible for different students, by different routes, to achieve these results.

All of the arts can be taught formally. The students are then enabled, not to produce, but to appreciate and understand great creations by masters of the field. The teaching here is not by trainers or coaches, but by intellectuals who communicate through concepts, theories, and principles, thereby making evident what it is that governs creation and enjoyment. Such teaching is now being carried on in many department and courses. Almost all colleges have, at different places on the campus, courses in the history of music and in the history of painting and sculpture; they always offer a history of English and French literature, and sometimes they make room for the history of classic, German, and occasionally other literatures. In each of these something is done that is not done in the others, but there is much that they share in aim and in content. It is unfortunate that the fact is not widely recognized; if it were, a number of courses would be brought into relation with one another, some current overlapping would be discovered, and what they all failed to cover would be made evident.

Ideally, all the histories are interested in individual works and in their temporal and cultural settings. But different types of history have different objectives, and use somewhat different methods. In a history of fine art, the styles, trends, schools, periods, and something of the accompanying environment and conditions come into focus. But in the classics, the history of English literature, and foreign languages, there is a greater concentration on learning how to read particular works, appreciatively and critically. Sometimes, to be sure, the emphases are interchanged, but whether they are or not, we are left with a number of different types of history.

The philosopher of art (no less than the historian of philosophy) is a philosopher whose interests differ from those of the historian or the teacher of art. Concerned with the categories and problems involved in creativity, he takes as his primary task the provision of ways in which multiple approaches and works can be brought within a single, unified, evaluative scheme. That scheme, and the principles which govern the making of a work of art, may not be known to other thinkers or to those who make works of art. Yet a knowledge of them enables one to do some justice to what is now in the process of being produced, and what the student will later confront.

If we are dissatisfied with merely adjusting the student to the accepted past, if we do not want to leave him unprepared for the present that is in the making or for the future that is to be made, we must convey to him the essence of art, its basic intent, its categories, and its references. We will then help him to be a man in the future and will prepare him to understand why it is that the arts of the past are enjoyable in the present—an end to be achieved by making evident how art portrays a reality which was there yesterday and will be there tomorrow. Art places the artist and the spectator directly before existence, as at once turbulent and law-abiding, threatening and serene, cosmic in reach, and at the center of everything. The well-taught student of the arts consequently knows in and through the arts what it is to be in a world far larger, much longer lasting, and much more powerful than that embraced by his society. And this surely is eminently worth knowing.

5]

Art is concerned with man in relation to realities which have a wider scope and more basic justification than could be provided by this world. Anthropology, sociology, psychology, politics, and religion can be characterized in similar ways. The first two, and often the third, can be brought together to constitute a single "social science." But whatever reasons may be advanced for bringing these together will also apply to the study of politics and religion. They too are "social sciences."

The thoughts, emotions, and acts of individual men are governed by laws which pertain to all. It is the task of psychology to make evident just what these laws are, and what man is because of them. But this is rarely acknowledged today in any but highly tendentious ways. Despite the fact that there are many schools of psychology in this country, most psychologists seem to be behaviorists. In the attempt to avoid the unverifiable suppositions of their predecessors, behaviorists make a strenuous effort to attend only to observables. Consequently they attend only to what happens when living beings are subject to certain conditions. Minds, intentions, drives, satisfactions are taken by them to be inaccessible and perhaps nonexistent; no reference to these supposed unobservables is to be permitted. Carried out, the idea is suicidal, for it denies that we should or can make any reference to potentialities or capacities. Yet no being can be subject to a condition unless it *is able to be subjected* to the condition. If it does not have the potentiality for being subject to the condition, it cannot be subject to it. In order to explain how a being can function behavioristically, the behaviorist inevitably, therefore, makes reference to the beings' abilities to be subject to the conditions to which they will respond. He evidently presupposes what his theory will not allow him to affirm.

Every psychologist must accept at least one all-encompassing potentiality, definitive of a single living being's readiness to function as a unity. The difference between a behaviorist and his opponent is essentially between one who is unwilling and one who is willing to speak of that potentiality. Since both psychologists do attend to specific forms of behavior, both take account of a number of subordinate potentialities as well. The behaviorist, because of his unwillingness to mention the limited potentialities which he presupposes and in terms of which he is experimenting, is also unable to explain differential behavior since this requires an explicit reference to these subordinate potentialities.

Psychology deserves a place in the curriculum, not because it tells us what living beings do, or how they think and learn, but because it teaches us what powers are native to living beings and how a plurality of activities can be understood to be the outcome of steady dispositions made subject to different conditions. No one of the dispositions is exhausted in any finite set of cases. To be interested in psychology is therefore to be interested in something not fully manifest, but which will help one to understand what in fact occurs.

Anthropology deals primarily with a complex of informal unstated relations which define a society as possessed of a single culture, tradition, mythology, and set of values. Sociology deals with more limited relations, and particularly those which prevail in the segment of the culture of the investigator. Today both enterprises are inclined to remain mainly with reports and statistics, so as to avoid the dogmatism and the unsupported generalizations and suppositions characteristic of the childhood of their subjects. But they cannot and they do not avoid making at least tacit use of principles of order and relevance, to thereby escape having only an unmanageable miscellany of items. And because they know the nature of man's potenti-

ality to be a public being they are able to know what a man
is, as well as the promise of his interaction with other men
and other realities. Both look away from man as he in fact
exhibits himself in past and present settings, to him as
capable of entering them. Like psychology, both enterprises presuppose and explicate the nature of what is not
yet entirely manifest.

The knowledge of the way in which men function as
individuals and in groups is justified by a knowledge of
what is potential. Yet we have no empirical means of
knowing what potentialities there are, except by studying
the shapes in which they have in fact been realized. If this
is true, we are forced to conclude that in anthropology and
sociology—and of course in psychology—we should study
what man has done, primarily because this will lead us to
know what he can do, and thus what he in fact constantly
is.

6]

Anthropology and sociology are rightly interested
in the roles which religion plays in the affairs of
men. Religious rituals, ceremonies, and even the affirmations of the religion are part of the cultures which these
subjects study. And the individuals who participate in a
religion—usually most of those who share in a culture—
have attitudes and ways of behaving which are appropri-
ately studied in psychology. Religion is a proper topic for
social science. This does not imply that religion is not a
distinctive subject with distinctive languages, objectives,
criteria, and achievements.

Anthropology, sociology, and psychology make evident the structure of the religious act, as well as the nature
of its power. They cannot however determine whether or
not what a religion claims is true or false; they do not and
cannot know whether or not its claims are justified or
legitimate, for they are unable to deal with it any but their

own terms. Religion, of course, reciprocates, taking them all to be instances of the way in which God is related to men, and the men are interrelated because of Him.

Religion is a distinctive activity in which men form a bond with one another by relating themselves severally and together to God, a power beyond them all. That God is present in religious men and in the communities they constitute. But though He is then in this world, He is not of this world, and the men and their communities are so far not of it either.

To justify the presence of religion in a curriculum of even the most secular college we must have it taught as a formal discipline. The students are then made aware that so far as they are involved in their daily world they are detached from God, and that only when they become detached from it can they be so involved with Him that they are able to return to their everyday world with an insight and inspiration acquired from that involvement.

To be religious is to engage in a distinctive practice. Such practice has no place in the school. Secular schools do not, and where dependent on public funds, may not teach the student to become religious. But this does not mean that he is not to be taught what the nature of religion is and what religion means to man. The practice of religion is an extracurricular matter to be carried out in church or home, but it should be and can be understood both in its main manifestations and as a generic or nuclear occurrence which those manifestations specify.

Religion properly taught in college tells about the nature and process of religion; it does not make students religious. When religiously-oriented schools refuse to tell students about other religions they in effect deny that those others have a dignity equal to their own. They are then like the secular schools which reject the teaching of religion as a formal study. Both fail to note the gap that separates the practice and the understanding of religion. The understanding is the understanding of the practice, a grasp of the distinctive way in which some men unite with one another, and thereby at once live with and under a God. That distinctive way is in fact specified in rather oppositional terms by the different religions. To know what religion is in fact, it is necessary to escape the limitations and stresses of each and every one of them, and to attend instead to the common factors that all of them exhibit. It is with these common factors that the student should become acquainted. But once again, this means that he must not only be shown how to turn from the daily world, but also from particular religions to what underlies them all and grounds whatever claims they warrantedly make.

7]

Courses in government or political science tell how states are constructed and function. These courses make use of descriptive material since they want to keep in contact with the actual processes and structures through which men are governed. But no description is more than an historic report, even when what is reported on is something which continues to operate. The student needs something else if he is to know how institutions are to be regulated and controlled, and what affect they have on man. He must approach them with some sense of what is just and reasonable, and thus in the light of the effect they ought to have. He must have some understanding of the objectives and duties of legislatures, of law-enforcement agencies, of administrative bodies, and of public-service boards. Otherwise he will be bogged down in the study of a morass of means, dealt with as though they were finalities. By being taught what states are and do, the student can come to understand somewhat better what they can and ought to do. He will then be better able to avoid repeating the mistakes of his elders. The most practical of disciplines has a place in a college curriculum only if it provides for the understanding of a side of it which may never become manifest in actual practice.

Democratic and communistic states diverge considerably in what they stress. The one defends civil rights at the price of considerable inefficiency, the other promotes efficiency and the importance of the state at the expense of individual rights. But both of them are only means, devices by which the eventual welfare and the happiness of man are to be achieved.

What is decided by politicians has an effect on everyone. This is not the same thing as to say that their decisions are of paramount intellectual importance. Politics can be as important as intellectual study as science and art and philosophy, but only so far as account is taken of the nature of the social good and the indispensable rights of man. It is a suitable subject for a college only if it attends to ideal situations which explain what is and what can be accomplished by a body of men. Properly taught it will enable the student to evaluate the justice of positive laws and the way in which they are applied, and thus to learn what ought still to be enacted and done.

8]

The curriculum of a college is routinely thought of as encompassing only formal subjects of instruction. The view is too well intrenched to make worthwhile a quarrel with it. But then it should be quickly remarked that if we speak in this fashion we must also say that a college program includes more than a curriculum. In any case, what is to be insisted on is that a college has two rather disparate parts in which the students are taught in quite different ways. The one enlightens the uninformed, the other habituates the unskilled. In one there is an emphasis on knowledge formally conveyed by teachers, and in the other—already touched upon in the discussion of art—there is an emphasis on training under the guidance of coaches. Where the formal side of a college breaks up into a plurality of subjects occupied with principles and concepts, the other divides into a plurality of activities occupied with training and the need to engage in responsible cooperative activities.

The difference between knowledge and training has been partly obscured by the usual distinction between the (humanistic) arts and the (exact) sciences. The first is thought to involve hardly any training, while the second is taken to require a considerable amount. But that distinction cannot be easily maintained. Students in the humanities are trained in reading and appreciation; students in the sciences acquire knowledge. Both the arts and the sciences are engaged in what can be formally known; both sharpen the students' critical acumen and stretch their imaginations.

The two types of enterprise differ mainly in methods, criteria, and results, the arts attending primarily to past insights and achievements where the sciences emphasize effective tools and methods. In modern times we have interchanged the meanings they once bore. In the arts division of most colleges (which do not always include the department of art) it is knowledge that is to the fore—but "science" is the traditional name for knowledge. In the science part of the college there is more of an interest in getting the student to produce something, to make something, to bring about a result—but this is quite close to what has been traditionally taken to be the objective of "art." The fine arts of music, painting, sculpture, etc., are evidently closer in spirit to the sciences than they are to the "arts" part of the typical curriculum, though they differ from both these arts and the sciences in their greater stress on doing and making, rather than on informing and manipulating.

Science, like the fine arts, can be formally taught. Attention is then paid to the nature of the principles which govern it, to its method, its historic achievements, and its place in civilization. The student is then informed, not trained; he thinks, but does not practice. As was true of the fine arts, science need not then be presented by masters who, through suggestion and correction rather than through the articulation of abstract truths, will help transform unskilled into disciplined practitioners. The student will be addressed by teachers, not drilled by coaches.

The youth, it was suggested, should be introduced to only one science, biology, taught primarily as an agency for forming his character. The young man, in contrast, can profitably study any one of the sciences. There is none from which he cannot learn how to make a disciplined use of what is already known. All are equally suited to enable him to begin a mastery of the methods, instruments, and skills to be employed in a controlled, independent inquiry.

A young man can be taught any science, but he cannot be taught all. No one has time enough for that. To which science should he be introduced? Will one be enough? Must he be taken beyond the elementary level, and involved in advanced work? These hard questions are often asked, but they are rarely asked or answered on a reasoned basis. Until they are, we obviously risk teaching what should be omitted, while omitting what should be taught.

Since the different sciences have different content to communicate, he who knows only one evidently knows only part of what it is desirable to know. But it is not the object of a college to make a student conversant with all that is worth knowing. Nor is it its object to turn him into a scientist. The main objective of science teaching is the development of the virtues of honesty, care, and self-control. Whatever course in science a student may take should make him aware of, and even help him to share in the spirit of scientific inquiry and to learn something of the structure of the laws of nature. If he can acquire the habit of observing with sensitivity, and inquiring and reporting responsively, cooperatively, and with precision, he will have begun to live as a mature man. These are grand objectives. They can be reached through the teaching of any one of the sciences.

In a first course in science a student should be made to

see how vital and creative a science is. One well-taught course in science, having this aim—even though it deals only with elementary experiments and principles—outweighs any number of professionally adroit but pedagogically dull displays of knowledge and skill. This fact is often obscured because most scientists treat first courses in science as occasions for introducing dead formulae, for repeating century-old experiments, and for retailing results of work done in the past. None of this is any more necessary than it is desirable.

As has already been suggested, the experiments which students should be shown and in which they participate need not be the watered-down, elementary investigations which now serve to bore them and their instructors in about equal measure. A student does not learn the nature of scientific experimentation by being given some trivial task or made to watch an imitation of some experiment by Galileo, Harvey, or Dalton. But he will learn it if allowed to watch a master go through a stage of his own investigation. Every experiment has multiple steps; almost all have some stage which can be performed before and explained to college students who have had no previous opportunity to see a science in process. It is some stage of the experiments in which the teacher is engaged that the student ought to watch and be allowed, in a limited way, to participate in. This will help him learn science (rather than something about it or something taken from it), and incidentally learn how to become clearer, more exact and exacting, and controlled.

All controlled inquiry can be said to be "scientific." But we are accustomed nowadays to designate as sciences only those enterprises which are interested in knowing the rationale that governs the empirically knowable cosmos. The exact sciences, even when their objects are confined to this globe—as may prove to be the case with botany and biology—are framed in terms of principles which are in principle applicable everywhere. It is because sociology, anthropology, and psychology do not range this wide—they deal, as we have already seen, only with man in limited settings—that it is a common practice to place them in a class by themselves. The separation is sometimes treated as a condemnation. There is no warrant for this, since these "social" sciences are pursued with the same care and precision as the "exact" sciences. Like the exact sciences they have their own distinct, testable methods by which they reach their own objectives, while cooperatively and dispassionately exercising judgment and control.

It is sometimes said that a genuine science should have a mathematical form. This demand need not be met. Indeed, it is not met in some eminently respectable sciences. Astronomy and geology have mathematical branches; they yield to mathematical treatment; but they also have non-mathematical branches where description and classification are the main objectives. And not only do the social sciences have both mathematical and nonmathematical branches, but literature, music, painting, and dancing can be divided in similar ways.

Nor is it true that all the sciences are experimental. There is no experimentation to speak of in astronomy and there is very little in geology. And though psychology is not usually included among the exact sciences, it does experiment. A man can be a great scientist and engage in little or no experimentation. Newton, Darwin, Einstein—to mention only the most conspicuous—speculated and inferred. They were not experimenters mainly, but thinkers, men occupied with illuminating principles having wide application. Still, experiment is a vital part of most scientific investigation and should, without having its importance or role distorted, be made a focus of the student's learning.

It is perhaps even more common to maintain that a science makes verifiable predictions. But were we to think this contention through we would have to deny that much of biology, astronomy, or botany is to be termed "scientific." And we would have some difficulty in finding a place for theoretical physics. This could be said to be predictive, but only if we treat its fundamental hypotheses, regarding the origin, limits, and fundamental constants of the cosmos, as definitions. And if this be allowed, we could in a similar way turn every enterprise into a predictive "science."

There are predictions in science, and these are more sharply formulated and are more often verified than any other attempts to say what will be. It is important for the student to learn why this is so, and how it is possible. It will be a rare student, though, who will get to the point where he himself can make predictions or where he can make intelligent use of them. We teach him more science, not by trying to show him how he can predict, but by conveying to him the distinctiveness of the scientific method, the laws which science has discovered, and the theories by which it explains those laws.

The exact sciences transcend the daily world to attend to mathematical realities or to speculatively known forces which govern whatever does occur. Their methods and principles are applicable throughout the cosmos; the theories they formulate and the laws they discover explain and bring order to the heterogeneity that characterizes the world of daily life. The student in learning about these realities and forces should then and there be made aware of the powers (and limits) of scientific inquiry.

Physics has a cosmic range and deals with elements to be found in every palpable thing. Its discoveries seem now to come at an accelerated rate. Many of them have clarified and helped explain what is known in other disciplines and in other ways. These facts apparently suffice to explain why almost all physicists and a good number of chemists, biologists, and geologists suppose that physics is *the* basic science to which all the others will eventually be reduced. But whether or not those who hold this belief can explain why it prevails, the belief, I am convinced, is not tenable.

Each science has its own distinctive problems, and is involved in procedures and results that are outside the purview, interest, or capacity of physics. Time for a biologist, for example, is something quite distinct from what it is for a physicist. Where physical time is serial, flat, and monotonous, the time through which an organism lives, and which paces its parts (as well as the whole of evolution), is accumulative and has an irregular beat. The chemist's ultimate elements, like the physicist's, are found throughout the cosmos. The physicist, though, discovers their nature and behavior in the course of an attempt to find comprehensive explanations for a plurality of laws, whereas the chemist deals with them primarily as confined within present, limited, and often palpable macroscopic objects. The complex elements which interest the chemist have quite distinctive properties, affiliations, and antagonisms, none of which are discoverable through physical means. Again, in physics, causation moves at the speed of light, whereas in geology the pace is so slow as to be almost imperceptible. These examples can be multiplied, but they suffice perhaps to make evident that there are a number of sciences, each with its own topics, to be pursued in distinctive ways.

He who knows only one of the sciences evidently has only a partial understanding of the nature of things and of the cosmos in which they are. But any one of the sciences can convey to the student the power of the scientific method, reveal the dedication that characterizes the scientists, and point up the inadequacy of common-sense interpretations and procedures. Instruction in any science puts the student on the road to acquiring a disciplined curiosity, a well-grounded imagination, and the ability to understand the world in abstract, universal terms—not too much to expect from a college student.

9]

Economics and engineering concern themselves with man's theoretical and actual involvement in the world. Both have distinctive practical and vocational bearings. Practical economics is the economics of the community, lived through as a business, and controlled by banks and monopolies and government, with an effect on everyone. A vocational school might teach it, thereby making it more likely that the students will be successful in the business and technological world. It is too useful a subject to be taught in college. We have no more right to teach it there than we have to teach proper breathing, standing, and walking. These too are important, but they are topics for a different time and a different place. We can justify the inclusion of practical economics in a college curriculum only if it is made to provide an opportunity for understanding the laws that govern the economic process. But then it must be taught by one who knows his economic theory.

Understood as including all the physical devices by means of which man controls and utilizes nature, engineering is the most characteristic enterprise of our time. Today is the age of the engineer. He articulates and controls our world on land and sea, above and below the earth. Because of the activities of scientists and their interest in the devices by means of which wars are won and space traversed, it is common to speak as though the engineer were engaged in scientific work. But he is not a scientist. Bombs and astronomical vehicles are not built by scientists but by engineers who take account of what scientists and mathematicians have already discovered. The scientific work was done a rather long time before, often without concern for the possible uses to which the scientific result could be put.

It is highly questionable whether engineering deserves a place in a college curriculum. It should be taught in specialized schools by specialized teachers on a par with those employed in medical, nursing, and law schools. A place can be found for it only if it be viewed as offering data and occasions where one can isolate general principles of structure and stress applicable in countless places and times.

Young men do not have sufficient experience or practice to enable them to forge sound judgments in practical affairs. They will though be caught up in them rather suddenly. If we want to prepare them for that day we must keep their attention focused elsewhere. College is the time and place to teach what has no practical use. Its appropriate subjects have their own intrinsic merit, illuminating and satisfying in ways no others do or can. They can in fact even be defended as the most practical of all subjects, since only they can be mastered without a long apprenticeship and yet allow one to share readily and fully in the spirit of civilization, and perhaps eventually to contribute to its growth and continuance.

10]

Apart from an occasional coach of a winning team, those who train young men to be proficient in sports are looked down upon by the academic community as little more than pariahs, hardly worth a nod. It is then made evident that our Greek inheritance has been forgotten or rejected, or that our colleges have been assumed to be simply continuations of the medieval universities.

It is only a slight exaggeration to say that Plato founded the first college and Aristotle the second. Their schools were attended by the wealthy, who cherished the manly virtues of courage, self-reliance, and sacrifice, rather than the scholarly virtues of precision, inquiry, and accumulation. The early medieval universities were mainly occupied with the preservation and communication of knowledge; they attracted not wealthy but dedicated students. The institutions which followed these once again appealed to the wealthy classes, and once again the gymnasium had a significant role to play in the education of young men.

The gymnasium and the field are proper parts of a college, fully coordinate with other parts. They should be open to all, the poor as well as the rich, the scholarly-minded as well as those who are not, and this without making the college into a factory turning out workmen for "professional" teams or entertainers for the alumni. We do sports and students an injustice, as Whitney Griswold, former president of Yale University, observed, when only a few young men are permitted to participate in sports, and then primarily in order to get them ready to perform in public for the pleasure of others. Sports then become the occupation of a gifted few and a spectacle for the rest. If the reason for teaching sports were kept in mind, more and more intramural sports would be offered until all students could participate in one or more of them. There are good indications throughout the country that this is an objective which is becoming increasingly favored.

In the gymnasium and the field the muscle tone is improved; there the students get needed exercise; there they are allowed to express and publicly sustain a desire for success, loyalty, and distinction. None of these desirable results is or ought to be the primary objective of sport, since none of them comes close to the core or promise of man. Sports are to be included in the college program because they build up the individual's sense of responsibility for doing excellently what he has committed himself to do, at the same time that they enable him to acquire the habit of cooperating with others. These virtues, when conveyed by coaches who are concerned with students rather than winning, can be acquired more readily and happily on the field and in the gymnasium than elsewhere.

To determine which sports should be pursued at a given stage of a young man's life, we must know the nature and powers of his body, the way it is best developed, and the way in which a sense of responsibility and a readiness to cooperate are most effectively inculcated. We are here on almost virgin territory, untouched by previous thought or reflection. We need a philosophy of sport. If it is built on a knowledge of what young men are like, what their capacities are, and what they need in order to grow most satisfactorily, it will help us at last to know if we now have too few or too many sports, and which new ones we might beneficially introduce.

11]

The elementary school prepares the student to fit into a part of a society. The secondary school fits him into a larger part, and helps him to profit from his presence there. The college helps him to become part of society as a whole, by enabling him to understand it in terms of the laws, categories, and principles that govern any kind of grouping of men.

The different types of school themselves constitute distinctive societies, within which are a number of separate subsocieties. In all, students make up one subsociety, the faculty a second, and administrators a third. There is some interplay among them, but this seems to have little effect on their characteristic rhythms, values, or development. And apparently it is possible to dispense with one or the other of them. In such a great institution as Harvard today, for example, students have little to do with or in their classes. Yet the educational process continues there with as much success apparently as is achieved in rival institutions, where the administration and faculty are more paternalistic and have some interest in teaching the young. From an educational standpoint the administration is obviously dispensable, but the illustration of Harvard would seem to indicate that the faculty also may not be as necessary to the educational process as it supposes itself to be. Teachers are not of great importance in a college where students are highly intelligent and very well motivated.

Students learn from one another in the dormitories, at mealtime, at parties, and in clubs. Nowhere is the student body either strong or evident enough to affect the spirit which pervades the faculty. And where the students constitute a strong subsociety of their own, the effect of teaching on them is rarely direct or noticeable. Fortunately, every once in a while a spark leaps across the barrier. It is this fact which makes some men continue to teach college students, desipte discouragement from the administration and the lack of evidence that conspicuous or lasting results are being achieved.

Some colleges are parts of universities having graduate and professional schools; most of the others feed into the universities, providing them with their most valuable graduate and professional students, and sometimes with their most effective teachers and distinguished scholars. Today both types of college tend to yield to university pressure and consequently take it to be their work to provide preliminary training and information for later studies to be carried on in the graduate or professional schools. As a consequence they are on the verge of losing their own integrity and therefore their roles.

The professional and graduate schools build on the college, but in different ways. The professional schools train men to become skilled members of the professions, with standards of excellence that have the approval of society. They help their students to master specialized skills for the sake of achieving social goods in ethical ways; their product, the professional man, thereafter submits to self-imposed ethical norms for maximizing efforts to promote social good. A graduate school instead introduces incipient teachers and investigators to new problems and

areas of knowledge, so that they can become masters and
contributors to the world that is about to be. The students
in both the professional and graduate schools should be
treated as members of a university, having something to
contribute to one another. But too often they are kept
separate. Were creative research treated as a profession on
a level with medicine, law, and theology, there would be a
greater tendency than there now is to have them enrich one
another.

A university is a combination of college, professional
schools, and graduate schools in equipoise, where men are
encouraged to sustain and contribute to the next major
turns of knowledge. Flanked by libraries, museums, and
workshops, it makes possible a leisurely and expert contact
with the basic and pivotal attainments of mankind. Such a
university is a unique American institution.

English universities have tended to neglect the graduate school and to concentrate on the college. Continental
universities have tended to neglect the college for post-
graduate work. These facts have not been widely noticed
because both types of university deal with highly selected
groups of students who are better prepared in their early
years than the Americans, and who are trained in the
professions throughout their university careers. The closer
an American university's practice approaches one of these
models, the more obvious the imbalance becomes.

An American University which has an English emphasis tends to be parochial, conventional, and conserva-
tive. If its emphasis is Continental, and particularly Ger-
manic, it tends to become technological, academic, and
disinterested in students. Today the small independent college leans toward the one, and the college in the university
leans toward the other. If the English and Continental
universities are to be used as models, they should be used
together, so that the failures of each are compensated for
by the successes of the other. A university is the universe
in miniature, filtered through a grasp of its reality and of

the main ways men have learned to deal with it. Nothing less than a combination of a self-respecting college and a graduate or professional school, manned by masters who convey the spirit of their subjects and the nature of the realities on which these depend, can bring men properly to the close of their formal education.

The college has the distinctive task of helping young men to participate in the basic values of the civilization of which their society is a part. Cutting back into the past and moving over the seas to other cultures, it enables them to become acquainted with the major attainments of mankind and to be alert to what is now beginning to be important in the new present. It should ready them to overcome those defects of their time which have been discovered in the course of a pursuit of world-wide and lasting truths. Through a teaching by mature men, who know their subjects and who can communicate not only the content but the spirit which animates them, the college fulfils young men as young men, here and now.

12]

All men, no matter how old or experienced, need to be educated. All are ignorant of some things and are undeveloped in some directions. There is no harm, however, in looking at education as primarily directed at the child, the youth, and the young man, and therefore as centered in the school—if only the work of the school is not completely separated off from all else, and if the process of maturation continues until the end of life.

Too often men tend to slight the process of education once they leave school. Yet the roughhewn world of everyday is only an awkward form of what is experienced in the ideal school. In the everyday world men continue to learn. But they do so by fits and starts, without much focus, rather haphazardly; they have neither plan nor organization, and are unable to answer to the exigencies of practical existence. They, no less than teachers and pupils, help define a school as a cage or a museum where a captive audience is made to attend to what has nothing to do with life, then or later.

Life in school is public life foreshortened and idealized; daily life is the world of the school overrun with irrelevancies. To stop the process of education merely because one has come to the end of a period of schooling is to begin a process of stagnation in contentedly offering old answers to new problems.

No matter how good the opportunities and the life, no matter how civilized and excellent one's community may be, it is necessary to continue to prepare oneself and others for new situations, tasks, and details. Otherwise the goods enjoyed will soon fade; eventually they will vanish. Even one who has had and continues to have a full joyous life must make some adjustments in order to continue in the new situations in which he inevitably finds himself. We must continue the process of education if we are not to fixate what we know, are, and can be, at some point in the past.

Some men immerse themselves as long as they can in the world of the school. They spend their days as administrators, principals, presidents, chairmen, and teachers. They can justify themselves only if they then promote the education, not only of students, but of themselves. Instead they tend to move into a pleasant, quiet, tidy world where they waste much of their own time and the time of others in details and trivia. Teachers who attend to the demands of current commerce or politics have no necessary advantage over the others, and certainly not over those who concentrate on classical languages, ancient history, or advanced mathematics. Teachers of supposed practical subjects can bore and stagnate as readily as those who teach other things. The only live subjects are those taught by live men.

It is not the task of the school to prepare the student to

lead a life that society endorses or rewards. It is not its function to enable him to be more efficient, more successful, or even better informed. Yet these are often explicitly, and even more often implicitly, taken to be the proper aims of the school. But then the true objective of formal education is obscured. Too soon one forgets that the purpose of education is to enable the student to live the best, the richest possible life, then and later.

The school provides instruments and opportunities for the living of a full human life. There training and discipline, knowledge and direction are offered; encouragement, criticism, and inspiration are there interwined. Joining a stress on accomplishment with one on drive, the school makes it possible to satisfy the needs of the student at a given stage of his career, while making provision for his arrival at a higher stage.

To enable a student to master a stage of learning appropriate to his present powers, needs, and situation, the school must provide appropriate material at appropriate times and in appropriate ways. It must offer goads, lures, stimuli, provocations; it must awaken interests and appetites when and as it satisfies. The well-taught student is so satisfied now that he is ready to be satisfied in another and better way later.

Too often our theories and practices have been concerned with achievement at the sacrifice of encouragement, or with drive at the sacrifice of present satisfactions. The young are sometimes satisfied but not prepared to move on to a higher level of study, or they are prepared for some higher level without proper regard for what they now are and deserve. Academic, and particularly progressive schools, tend toward the first of these extremes, while vocational, and particularly traditional schools, tend toward the second. Both fail to do all they can and should to help the student live a good life then, in such a way that he will eventually live a life worthy of a grown man.

In an ideal world, the student in college would be so

well motivated that one would be able to say to him: "You now have four years in which to find yourself. Take any courses you like. If you don't want to, you need not go to any classes, nor take any examinations. You need not even write an essay. But if you want to write one your teachers will help you with advice, suggestion, and criticism, pointing out your strengths and weaknesses." If the admissions committee has rightly chosen, the students will take advantage of their opportunities, and will therefore, at the end of four years, be ready to take up the burdens of responsible men. Though this answer cannot be carried out today, there seems to be no reason why we should not now try to approximate it.

The lives that men lead after they are graduated from school offer little evidence that they had been properly prepared for living. No signal reform of our schools can be expected until we are aware of the lives men lead, and why it is they ought not to lead them. Only then can we hope to alter current practices properly, and thereby make it likely that most men will make proper use of their spare time.

5

The Lives Men Lead

CIVILIZATION RESTS ON LABOR. In the past it has been the labor of men who were denied participation in the very world they made possible. Of this, most of us are acutely aware. We are alert today to the injustices on which the glory of Greece and the grandeur of Rome depended. Their division between the supported idle and the laboring man who worked for them, is now thought not to be desirable, though there still are those who need not work and those who can live only if they do.

Our creative artists, religious leaders, philosophers, scientists, and teachers are economically viable today. They are paid, some of them even more than those who drive trucks, build bridges, or work on the roads. And most men, no matter what their work, usually have considerable spare time in which a rich life can be lived. Today, both those who labor and those who do not are seen to be part of a single civilized world which they sustain and maintain, even though too many fail to find much in it that attracts or satisfies.

Most men are involved in a practical life—in production, in making the production possible, or in seeing that its outcome is known and used. The more successful usually exhibit some degree of native shrewdness, good practical judgment, considerable self-control, and an understanding of the impulses and drives of man. No one of these, nor all of them together, will of course enable a man to be successful. Much depends on luck. But those virtues are almost indispensable, and will protect and even increase the advantages that luck brings about. Nevertheless, he who spends his life making, exchanging, or storing up goods partly wastes that life. Our treasure may not be in heaven, but it also is not wholly in earthly goods.

Production is a necessity. It and its associated enterprises are in good part responsible for the great gap that separates primitive and modern life. But that does not imply that the lives devoted to it are altogether well-spent. And they will never be well-spent so long as they are not animated by the spirit of those who are occupied with final goods. Still, it is the active men who enable society to continue and perhaps to prosper. As a reward the men sometimes achieve a position of power—usually in the form of money, which is perhaps the most evident sign or instrument of power. The money enables them to participate in social activities, not only as producers but as purchasers. But in neither role are the men involved in the final activities of possession and consumption. As producers they make things primarily in order to have them sold and used; as purchasers they buy things preparatory to putting them to a final use. Both may be wasting their time. To determine whether this is the case or not, attention must be given to the value of what is finally owned and enjoyed. The end defines what is right and wise to do beforehand.

Work need not be tedious, stultifying, without compensation. There can be a pride in workmanship, a joy in seeing that something has been done excellently. Workmen can be craftsmen even when engaged on minor projects. Craftsmanship is the ennobling of means, the production of what, though attractive, is to serve some further end; it is workmanship at its best. This is never identical with art, where creativity is added to a concern for a final good. But the workman who shares in the attitude of the artist can be a maker of excellent means. Though he never produces the beautiful, he can produce the graceful.

Education is concerned with the mastery of finalities, not with training in the means by which these might be obtained. Yet our schools, even those most dedicated to the advancement of a liberal or humanistic program, devote most of their energies to directing students toward a life in the world of production. There would be much warrant for this if the purpose of education was the preparation of men for the lives most of them in fact will lead. But then we should boldly assert that our colleges are nothing more than high-grade vocational institutions. If this be so, where will students learn about the lives they ought to have? Where will they learn that which should quicken and inspire them then and later?

Factories, railroads, bridges, airplanes, museums, and libraries are only agencies by which goods may be made more accessible to man. No one who did not misconstrue the nature of man, and what he needs to do and be in order to fulfill his promise, would confuse such agencies with what they make possible.

2]

Not far from the world of economic affairs is that of government and politics. Indeed, they coincide at many points and overlap a number of times. Politics is often just business carried on in a roundabout way. Armies follow the balance sheet, and what they take over is soon protected by the police. But ideally, and sometimes in practice, the political life is occupied with its own problems which it works through with its own methods and for its own ends. It can be guided by an awareness of the goal that ought to be realized. That goal is peace, and the welfare and prosperity of a people, to be reached in part through law and the use and control of governmental machinery, the means by which men can function effectively together.

Peace for us has never been more than an interlude between wars, during which antagonisms flourish while preparations are made for an eventual use of weapons of destruction. And, up to now, there has never been a wholly prosperous people. But poverty has been reduced and in some areas abolished, and the welfare of all has become a consciously accepted goal for many nations. Throughout the world, countries have learned how to avoid extreme epidemics, and all now successfully restrain most public expressions or violence. But ours is not yet a world where many men at ease and in health are ready and able to enjoy what man at his best can be and do.

Government and its associated political forces are indispensable agencies by means of which we can attain and live a good life. They affect everyone and are somehow shared in by all. This is perhaps why politicians say that they are the servants of the people, though they do not often seem to remember that servants relieve their masters of their burdens to make it possible for them to live long and well.

Necessary for the good life, political agencies are not sufficient for it. When the agencies have done their work, men are still faced with the problem of living in that civilized life that politics should have made possible and should sustain.

3]

Lives devoted to service—in the "services," the hospitals, churches, and schools—would seem to be more significant than those which are spent in production or in governmental activities. Because those who serve build on these others and make use of what these provide, so as to improve the lot of man, most people would take such lives to be superior in content as well as in dignity to those spent in business, manufacture, or politics. There is a tendency too to think that those who devote themselves to service have nobler motives, are essentially unselfish, and produce what is eminently desirable. This may be true quite often, but there are outstanding exceptions. The motives, interests, and achievements of those engaged in production or government, moreover, are not infrequently of a high order, while some of those involved in service sometimes have highly questionable motives. If one type of life is superior to the other, it is because it aims higher and accomplishes more. Only when viewed in this way does it become apparent that a life of service, since it focuses more on man, his rights, his needs, and his satisfactions than production or government can or does, is on the whole superior to lives devoted to them.

Production is too much involved in the process of making things, while political activity is too much occupied with the rules, regulations, structures, laws, compromises, and power (which make effective public action possible), to be able to attend sufficiently to what men need and deserve. A life of service, in contrast, even though occupied with removing obstacles and with the provision of opportunities, is humanly centered and ready to be alert to individual needs and problems. Still, no less than production and government, it is occupied mainly with means. A life of service cannot therefore be truly said to be a genuinely good life.

A man needs a steady public order, bodily and mental health, and guidance and instruction before he can be all that he should be. It is desirable that these be provided, but it would be regrettable were we content to rest with these, or were we to suppose that a life devoted to them was a life as rich as a human life could be.

4]

A better life, indeed the only life worthy of a man, Aristotle and many other thinkers have claimed, is one which primarily or centrally involves the use of the mind. Man's mind they say is his most distinctive feature, separating him from the brutes. It is because he has a mind that he most resembles a god, one who is able to contemplate the pure and fixed essence of whatever there be. The thesis I think cannot be maintained unless it be qualified considerably. Men sometimes use their minds in regrettable ways; their minds may be filled with trivia, or they may dwell on the vulgar, the demeaning, the evil, and the despicable. Men can use their minds for the devising of means for undesirable ends; their ideas can be distortive and corrupt. Nor need the human body be treated as a base vessel, the place where man is one with the brutes. A man can use his body in such a way that his character is developed and grace and graciousness are exhibited.

A mature man has a disciplined body as well as a disciplined mind, backed by a controlled expression of the emotions and will. A life centered about the use of the mind is too thin and narrow to be worthy of a man. And if it be the case that finite and empirical knowledge is the avenue by which one reaches an understanding of the basic realities and truths that underlie all else, the life of the mind, as it is usually followed, will also be a life involved only with means.

5]

Production, political activities, service, and cognition offer significant, desirable avenues through which a man can express high motives and achieve important results. But no one of them provides for as complete a life as a man can and ought to have. They are all too earthbound, too self-centered, too narrow-gauged, and too remote from the core of man's being and need to allow them to do justice to his powers and expressions. We must look elsewhere if we are to know what kind of life a man ought to live.

Public leaders, religious thinkers, and psychiatrists think they know. They tell us that a man ought to lead the fullest, richest possible life. Unfortunately, though not un-

expectedly, they differ in their description of it, as well as
on the question of how and when it is to be attained.

Public leaders seem to have as their goal the production of unique, private beings, but they also seem to want
to defer the achievement of this for a while. Full attention,
they think, should now be given instead to the production
and maintenance of a public, peaceful, and prosperous
order. This, it is hoped, will make the desirable outcome
possible or even inevitable. It would be a mistake to follow
their lead, for we would then occupy ourselves with what
is not in fact known to promote a desirable end. No public,
peaceful, prosperous order will make certain that we will
thereupon get something else, particularly if all the while
we had neglected a concern for other values and tasks.
After the rejected have had their civil rights returned to
them, and have been given medical care, jobs, and opportunities to rise in the social and economic scale, they and
all the rest will still be faced with the problem of how to
live a good life.

Were we, with the religious leaders, to concern ourselves with the attainment of a nonworldly goal, we would
not only have beliefs, values, and objectives which some
men find dubious, and which are certainly questionable,
but we would not yet have made adequate provision for our
living a good life here and now. It is characteristic of all
Utopias, religious and otherwise, to allow the glory of the
day-to-come to blind them to some of the misery of the men
who are now defeated by others, and often by themselves
as well.

Psychiatrists are concerned with a good life to be lived
here and now. They think it is attained when men function
smoothly inside an established society. It is of course a
good objective for men, were there ideal societies and no
need to satisfy private interests or demands. But all societies are imperfect; some are seriously defective and corrupt; no one of them does justice to man's sense of beauty
or to his search for truth. A man cannot be said to be

greatly helped as an individual, if all that is done to help him is to make him fit a little better inside whatever society is available. If he were content to become an excellent part of any actual society, he would succeed in doing nothing more than to allow himself to be an efficient part of an undesirable whole. This fact prevents us from looking to psychiatrists to learn what the good life is, and therefore what we ought now to do to attain it.

Our society does not necessarily offer the best possible context for any of us. It functions without much plan; its progress and aims are skewed by folklore, conventions, superstitions, habit, and intrenched powers and privileges. Fortunately, there are other and higher goals than that of being a good member of it, or even of the best of societies.

Education is the process by which men are enabled to live the fullest possible life that is open to them at each stage. The last stage is maturity, when men can be maximally fulfilled. An educator should know the main features of that stage, whether or not it has many distinctive, subordinate forms, and how it can be most readily realized. Unless he knows at least this much, he will not know in what direction students should be pointed, what courses are to be required of them, and in what order those courses should be taught and how. Only that educational theory which knows what is best for mature men will be able to avoid losing focus and direction; only it will be able to justify its choices and selections.

Too often educators are content to follow the lead of public figures, religious leaders, or psychiatrists, or to adopt something like their attitudes toward ends and means. Inevitably educators then urge activities not altogether appropriate to man's promise and aspiration. To compensate for this error, and helping to hide that error from themselves, the educators are inclined to spend much of their energy in the development, promotion, and use of educational techniques. But these techniques, no matter how well tested, and no matter how effective, will have a

questionable value if not directed at realizing a desirable
end. The best of techniques in such a case may in fact
prove to be only a most efficient device for going where one
ought not to be.

Perhaps there are no ends at all? Were that the case
there would be nothing to plan for; we would have lost all
reason for directing or educating men. The same consequence follows if there be as many good ends as there are
men. But might there not be a limited number of final
ends? There might. But then we must break up the human
race into a plurality of distinct classes, all of which would
presumably be on a footing with one another. This is a
possible and perhaps even a plausible supposition. But it
cannot finally be maintained, for it does not do full justice
to the fact that all men are part of a single mankind and
that each one ought and can realize a common end in a
distinctive way.

Men form multiple classes, in each of which the members share traditions, backgrounds, hopes, appetites, desires, and values, and where they face a distinctive common goal. The members of the different classes are also
members of mankind and, so far as they are, face a single
common human end. That single common end is specialized as the distinctive goals for the men in their different
classes. Since each man is a distinct individual with unique
experiences and values, we must also add that each deserves to live out a common end, as well as specialized
forms of it, in a manner unlike that lived by another.

The common end for man, satisfying basic needs and
fulfilling human promise, must be made relevant to and be
reachable by everyone. It must complete a man, making
use of his distinctive powers for growth in range, and a
mastery of himself and his instruments. It should benefit
from his creativity and appreciation, and dictate what else
he does and ought to do. Its pursuit need not and should
not stop with formal instruction in the college or university, since this can do no more than bring some men to the

point where they can individually live in and with a good that is open to all.

Fortunately, all of us have some intimation of the nature of the final good for man. Expressed generally enough it is one to which most would quickly subscribe. Unfortunately, when we identify and describe it, we tend to overparticularize and make it seem somewhat limited. This is one of the reasons why it has been identified and described many times in the past, in not altogether compatible ways.

6]

Again and again we hear claims to the effect that pleasure, wealth, power, fame, or security is the end which men should realize. All these have initial plausibility, but no one of them I think can withstand critical scrutiny.

There are good pleasures and bad pleasures, pleasures which enhance and pleasures which weaken. Indulgence in liquor or food, highly pleasurable though these be, have inescapable terminal points. Beyond those points, pleasure diminishes and then ceases altogether. Even before it satiates, it can become a bad pleasure, a pleasure which precludes further pleasure. Those who desire to make pleasure the highest of ends cannot be referring to these, but must instead be referring only to *good* pleasures. But to obtain good pleasures, it is necessary to spend time estimating consequences and in selecting and controlling acts and desires. If pleasure be our goal, we must sometimes forego it to make it possible. Indeed, there are occasions when we may have to deny ourselves *any* pleasure for a while so that the good pleasure can be assured at some later time. Also, there are pleasures of the mind as well as of the body. These are achieved, not by attending to possible pleasure, but to the needs of an inquiry or a discipline. It is of course possible to be interested in them for the sake of the pleasure they might provide, but they are more likely to satisfy only if one engages in them because one wants to learn and to know. We obtain most pleasure, not by making pleasure a goal to be sought and achieved, but by getting it in the guise of a surplus value attaching to something else.

A man might want to learn and to know, not only to avoid the pain of not knowing or of not learning, but in order to obtain the contrasting pleasure. If so, he can be sure only of being disappointed. There is no unalloyed pleasure in learning or knowing. Honest inquiry is riddled with doubt and difficulty. All learning involves struggle. To learn and know we must subject ourselves to criticism by ourselves and by others. The supposed pain of not knowing or of not learning is in fact rarely as acute as is the pain of frustration or the pain of discovering that one has been on the wrong track for quite a while. We learn and know, not because learning and knowing are pleasurable in themselves nor because they promote the most pleasure, but because we dislike being ignorant, even when the ignorance is pleasant, the learning painful, and the knowledge disagreeable.

Normally when we learn and know, we find ourselves somehow enriched, at peace, completed. This is because learning and knowing are part of a desirable end. On attaining that end, in whole or part, we are usually suffused with a feeling of satisfaction. This is a state of pleasure, but one that is quite distinct in quality, quantity, cause, and outcome from sensuous pleasure. And whether that desirable feeling be called pleasure or not, like most rich and satisfying pleasures it is only an incidental product of the satisfaction of a concern, not for pleasure, but for something else—in this case, learning and knowledge and what these help constitute.

Men who give themselves to a life of pleasure are few in number. Pleasures are individual occurrences, terminal and transitory, existing only when and as they are being

enjoyed, consumed, and lived through. Men are often foolish but not many are so foolish that they occupy themselves
with the pursuit of such ephemera.

Many men devote themselves to the accumulation of
wealth. For this there is some warrant. Wealth has a
bearing on others, and has a tendency to remain with those
who acquire it. It enables its possessor to avoid many
frustrations and limitations; it gives him prestige; it en-
larges his powers and extends his influence. It also provides him with some pleasure and with a means to obtain
other pleasures for himself and those in whom he is interested. He who acquires wealth usually finds too that he has
the happy feeling that he is a favored child of fortune. He
and others more often than not take the wealth to provide
testimony, moreover, that he is intelligent, shrewd, and
disciplined. This list of benefits can be extended. But it is
sufficient to make evident that the possession and retention
of wealth is partly due to exterior factors, and that it is
desirable, not in and of itself, but as grounding or allowing
for other goods. Wealth at the very best can be only a
condition for reaching a desirable end.

Wealth can never be more than a means. That it is a
necessary means to the final end is a not unheard of claim.
But it remains an ungrounded claim until one can show
that none but the wealthy ever are or can be perfected men.
The evidence and the prospects are all the other way. He
who is concerned with wealth must attend to multiple
contingencies, or risk losing his favorable position. Such
concern precludes the extended enjoyment or pursuit of the
arts and the sciences, and other goods of civilization; it
allows little or no time to be spent in a participation in the
making and promotion of a civilized life. It is no surprise
therefore to find that men who are primarily concerned
with wealth are usually untrained and undisciplined spec-
tators of both the arts and the sciences. Even they themselves sometimes sense that they are far from living the
best of lives.

It is a mistake to devote one's time and energy entirely or primarily to the having or to the acquisition of wealth, unless the final end is thereby automatically obtained. And this, the empty lives of some men of wealth show, is not the case. Riches of course do not preclude the existence or use of the imagination, insight, creativity, or intelligence. An artist or scientist might be a rich man. Cézanne said that his father did him the very great service of leaving him with money enough to allow him to paint without thought of the morrow. But the wealth here is obviously not an end but an instrument for making that end realizable. Millions of Americans, Frenchmen, Germans, and Japanese *can* be wrong; no one ought to be primarily concerned with making or having money.

One of the ends which wealth might be thought to promote is power. He who has money is able to control much of the machinery of existence. He can sometimes place himself in a position of authority, and direct and even rule other men. He is freer than most to move, to act, and to speak. Such power is good to have. A man at his best approaches the position of a truly free and powerful spirit, at once unconfined by the world and able to make it function as he desires. Because he is then most like a god, he who has power over things and men is thought to be most truly a man.

Power need not depend on wealth for its existence. It is in fact possible for the wealthy to find themselves restricted and confined, unable to exercise the power which the wealth was expected to provide. The comparatively poor can instead be in the ascendant. Priests and sages, bureaucrats, politicians, artists, teachers, soldiers, or policemen can sometimes be in greater control both of things and men than the richest of men may find it possible to be, since the money and its accompanying power may not be readily available, appreciated, or submitted to.

Power often has overtones of pleasure. It, like wealth, also brings prestige. It too seems to testify to the presence of unusual virtue. But like wealth it is not and cannot be more than a means to some end. Indeed, it is only that common factor in different means by which one is enabled to move to an end. Wealth is power precisely because and so far as it is an effective means; reputation is power precisely because and so far as it is an effective means; love is power precisely because and so far as it is an effective means. Technology, economic prosperity, and productivity are public forms of power, and are so only because and so far as they are effective means by which we can move to where we ought to be.

To have power is not necessarily to have wisdom or even intelligence enough to use it well for oneself or for another. Power, because it is only a means, can promote what ought not to be, even for those who possess and exercise that power. There is therefore no reason to believe that he who has power will himself arrive, or will enable others to arrive where they want to go or ought to be. And men, as we all have learned, can and sometimes do use power to injure, debase, and destroy themselves and others. To avoid this consequence, one must know how to control and use power in such a way as to produce what is good. This, because it is an end, cannot be more power—for this is still a means—but must be something else.

He who has status satisfies an apparently almost insatiable desire to be accepted, acknowledged, and approved; its highest form is evidently fame. This is more like an end than power is, particularly since it often provides one with a power that can be most effectively used for oneself and others. It also offers the only form of immortality which one can be confident that a man can have. More important, fame testifies both to the fact that a man has an appreciated nature or career, and to the fact that others publicly endorse what he is or has done.

All apparently desire fame. Even he who works at some unglorious task, who occupies himself with what has only a momentary significance, or who cuts himself off from the world and its values, both needs and wants the good will of others. He would like to be the object of their good opinion. He would like to be remembered by others for what he really is. He too wants to be famous, though not in the usual way, for fame is testimony that he has done what should be done and is the man he ought to be.

Fame translates a man's nature and accomplishments into values and judgments made by others. These values and judgments however may be indifferent to what he in fact is, or to the merit of what he has done. Fame offers testimony, but this may be neither accurate nor sufficient. It offers only an unreliable guide to merit and desert, because it is external to the self. It may not come to those who deserve to be well-known; it may be directed at aspects of them which have been misconstrued. Instead then of fame being the end we seek, it but provides us with a not altogether reliable indication that we are deserving of admiration, presumably because we are as men ought to be.

Perhaps every man has a hope or expectation of fame. So far as he is assured that the hope or expectation is well-grounded, he finds himself supported and reassured, perhaps even justified; he is a man who does what he ought to do and is what he ought to be. If the fame comes early enough, it may renew his confidence that he is someone of distinction. But even where the fame justly celebrates virtues and deeds of evident renown, it will not necessarily offer evidence that the individual has lived a good life. Conspicuous virtue and great deeds are possible to men who are confused, whose vision is limited, whose tastes are perverse, whose spirits are shallow, and whose lives are bare.

The secure man is able to maintain himself against the threat and the fact of destruction, to withstand the actual invasion of his privacy, and to defeat the denial of his rights and beliefs. At last he can be himself at the same time that he is harmonized with his fellows. It is sometimes thought therefore that man's proper end is the achievement and continuation of security.

Security is desirable. It is good to possess oneself in onself, and thereby be protected from the dangers which beset everyone every day and on every side. But one can become secure at a point short of where one ought to be. Security is desirable only in the form of a protection of the goods we have already attained and for assuring the use of means for attaining further goods. In the end it therefore can be only a condition for getting the result men ought to achieve. What is this? I think it is the correlative of a man, to possess which is to be complete. It evidently cannot be known until we know what it is to be a complete man.

7]

All men make distinctive demands, expressing their distinctive powers and needs. These powers and needs are so many different ways in which men can act to bring about distinctive results. Until their demands are satisfied men remain unfulfilled, only potentially what they can be.

The demands are of at least three kinds—bodily, mental, and emotional. Some of them are expressed primarily through the body, some through the mind, and some through both together. Some impede and some support other demands. Often they conflict with one another. What the mind entertains is not always in accord with what the body needs or has; the emotions have rhythms and an insistence of their own. A perfected man is one whose mind, body, and emotions have their distinctive promises fulfilled in harmony with one another, while he is in harmony with other similarly perfected beings.

The good life is the achievement of one who, having found a center in himself, and while making primary use of some power, say that of his mind, allows other powers some play. When he does this, he becomes a good person, one who acts well habitually. Since his opportunities and abilities are restricted in range, and yield less than he needs, he must also contribute to and participate in the achievements of all the others. Men must be fulfilled together if they are to be fulfilled severally.

Education is the art of producing fulfilled men. These are men who have lived up to their promise, and who therefore contribute to and share in the funded wisdom and achievements of mankind. Such education takes one beyond the school to a world where work and play are governed by values that have been discovered and produced in leisure—a period which has too often been confused with idleness or recreation, and therefore has not received the attention it deserves.

6

Leisure Time

BECAUSE LEISURE TIME has not often been sufficiently distinguished from quite different periods, it is desirable to begin with some definitions. *Spare time* is that portion of the day that is not used for meeting the exigencies of existence. *Idle time* is a spare time in which nothing of value is accomplished; it is an empty time, a time which just passes away. *Recreational time* is a spare time in which one is refreshed, relaxed, re-created, and thereby enabled to work better, with renewed interest, strength, and efficacy. *Leisure time* is spare time in which one pursues and enjoys final goods.

No one has spare time who cannot dispose of time as he will. Infants, the gravely ill, and those just managing to live on a subsistence level have no spare time. All their energies are devoted to the task of living. Slaves of the life they live, their rest or play are only occasions for recuperation and preparation, pauses in a single activity.

The rich and many of uninstitutionalized recipients of public charity have maximum spare time. They need spend only a minimum period on tasks essential for the continuation of a healthy existence. Most of their day is unrequisitioned by nature or society. It is theirs to waste in idleness or to spend in some enriching activity.

Most men have spare time somewhat below the maximum. Its amount depends on two factors—what they accept as necessities, and the circumstances in which those necessities are to be provided. Because men differ on what it is to be a man they differ on what they accept as necessities. An unnecessary luxury for one is an indispensable requirement for another. And because they are subject to different pressures and are confronted with different opportunities one man will have a great deal of spare time when another may have none at all.

We all live in a society, in various subdivisions of it, and in terms of some peer group—of which we may not be a member. Depending on where we are or aspire to, existence makes different demands on us. If the times are unpropitious the demands on us may be few and minimal and yet take up all our thought and energy. In periods of peace and ease, the demands men feel called upon to meet increase in range and number without necessarily affecting the length of their spare time. But in war, in crises, when cataclysms overwhelm, it may take an entire day to meet the minimal needs that a day's bare living defines.

Sometimes it is thought that maximum spare time can be made available by providing the most favorable conditions for satisfying bodily needs. Such an approach has the advantage of making use of a single, universally applicable idea of man—that of a biological being. It also provides a perceptive concept of the demands of existence (what is needed in order that men may live in health), and a comprehensive and flexible meaning for leisure time (the time that remains after bodily needs have been satisfied). It also allows one to see that no matter how precious the goods of civilization are, they are not as necessary for a man's being as are food and drink, shelter and rest. Still, it would be foolish to overlook the fact that a man has a mind and a will as well as a body; that he has emotions, drives, ambitions, and hopes; that he has a personality which needs direction and deserves development; and that he has potentialities which he should actualize if he is to be a whole man.

A man has intellectual, spiritual, and emotional as well as biological needs. Strictly speaking, he has spare time only after the minimal conditions for having and using a genuine human mind, personality, self, and body have been satisfied. Unfortunately, no one knows just what these minima are, and since so few people do anything to show that they have and use not only a body, but a mind, personality, and self as well, comparatively few could then be said to have any spare time at all.

Because men set different values on what is available after the bare means of subsistence have been provided, they have different minima which they think must be met before they can take themselves to have any spare time. However, they differ on these questions more as members of various social classes than as individuals. Similarities in age and education, financial condition, and interest tend to bring them together in classes, where they exhibit a concern for common values not of primary interest to members of other classes. Their spare times begin at different points.

The set of indispensable necessities for one laborer is somewhat like that of another's. Their ages, education, financial state, and general interests, and therefore their necessities, have somewhat the same range. Most executives are older, have more education, are financially more secure, and have wider interests than laborers. Many things that the laborers ignore are for the executives essential parts of a minimal standard of decency. Only after these have been acounted for, do the executives feel that they have time to spare. Nevertheless, the amount of spare time for both classes might be more or less equal, precisely because each acknowledges distinctive necessities above the bodily that must be met before spare time is available. In that spare time they will of course then go on to do quite different things.

The problem of obtaining spare time is in root the problem of the allocation of only part of one's day to necessary work. This each individual can determine for himself, once he excapes from circumstances which require him to devote all his time to providing necessities for his type of life.

With the abolishment of slavery, child labor, and peonage, with the increase in protective devices, the destruction of the sweat shop, the introduction of a shorter workday and shorter workweek, social security, annuities, and pensions, almost all working men have a greater amount of spare time available to them than their parents had. Some, without appreciable gain in ability or opportunity, set their sights higher than their parents did, and as a consequence have less rather than more spare time at their disposal. Some of them even spend their energies trying to meet the minimal conditions of a life beyond their capacities, and are therefore without any spare time. Others get into a somewhat similar state because, though less gifted than their parents were, they aim just as high; while a few others, having settled for a life more limited than their parents', find themselves with a great deal of spare time, even though circumstances may not be much different for them than they were for their parents. The children of moderately successful immigrants sometimes take this last alternative. They abandon the ambitions of their parents to settle for their achievements, thereby making possible a greater amount of spare time.

2]

Spare time can be used up in idleness. It can also be converted into leisure time. That time is not empty. Leisure is a period filled with activity, mental and physical, carried on in a spirit of ease and self-sufficiency, whose values are to be imported into whatever work one might subsequently engage in.

Most often leisure time is identified with recreational time. But in recreational time men are made ready, through relaxation and rest, for work or idleness. Leisure time instead is made possible by work; it is not a time in which work is made possible.

Leisure time is a spare time subject to two restrictions. It does not preclude the performance of necessary work. If it did, it would be self-defeating, since work makes it possible. But it is also not to be used for the sake of making men work better. Leisure is not a time to prepare for work, itself a means to some other end, but rather a separate period in which one may "work" hard, but not at that which has value only because it is economically useful, politically desirable, or widely desired.

What one does in leisure time may have economic, political, and social consequences of a high order; work that is done after a period of leisure time may gain much from what was then done. But the leisure time is spent not with an eye on these, but on final goods. Leisure time, a time free from work and necessities, is essential for the attainment of anything of fundamental value. Not a time to be filled out somehow, not a time to enjoy simple pleasures, leisure is that time when a man enriches his life by building on what he had been enabled to possess through education.

Etymologically "school" and "leisure" are one. There is warrant in this identification, for in both we can deal with finalities since we are there freed for a time from the need to make a living. Both allow us to live in a world held apart from that hurly-burly, vexatious bustle that characterizes much of our daily existence.

What school is for the student, leisure time is for the mature. When an educated man arrives at the point where he has leisure, he can at last move to the position of being wise. Only then will he live a full life, a life in which he gives meaning to what had gone before and whatever work he might do.

3]

It is possible to be freed from the pressures of daily life and still not have leisure time. This occurs when a man has no interest in leisure or no ability to make use of spare time. It occurs too when he is subject to conditions that are not propitious, or when he lacks the facilities which would enable him to express his interests, make use of his abilities, and take advantage of the conditions.

There are some men so absorbed in the activities of daily practical life, that they have no interest in anything else. They have no hobbies and no curiosity. They want to keep themselves occupied in what they always do. Given a shorter workday or workweek, vacations, release from duties, they become depressed and unhappy, awaiting the passage of time so that they can return to their work. Spare time is for them a burden, something to be feared and rejected.

There are others who have sufficient interest in matters which can be pursued only in spare time, but who lack the capacity or ability to engage in these. Interested in reading, they are comparatively illiterate; interested in new experiences, they are somewhat timid or unimaginative. As a result they become frustrated. Spare time for them is a period of exposure, and sometimes of self-discovery, when they become anxious, anguished, and defeated, gaining little except an awareness of their limitations and comparative inferiority.

It is possible to have both the interest and the ability to make use of spare time, and yet be prevented by circumstance. Interested and able to fish, the weather may not be suitable, or there may be no lake or river nearby. Interested and able to enjoy the theater, they may be too far from a playhouse or theater group.

Interest, abilities, and conditions may all be adequate and still no leisure time may in fact be available because there are no facilities making its use possible. The fisherman needs his rod and net; the musician needs his score and instrument. It is foolish of course to provide these facilities for men who have neither an interest nor an ability to make use of them, or to provide them under conditions that make their use difficult or impossible. But it is cruel to refuse to provide facilities for men interested and able to make more than a minimal use of their surplus time and energies.

A realistic program regarding the use of leisure time takes account of the nature of men's interests and abilities, what it is that the conditions permit, and what facilities can and will be offered. But since it is true that not all interests are equally valid, all men fully developed, all conditions equally desirable, or all facilities readily obtainable, it is essential that such a program be guided by an idea of the proper objective to be obtained through the best use of the time.

Spare time can be best used only if some spare time is spent in preparing for leisure. The awareness, for example, that man's interests need refinement, expansion, and direction, points up the necessity for adult education. That program involves an incursion into available spare time. And since men need training in the proper exercise of their powers if they are to make profitable use of the time available, they must also use some of their spare time in order to get ready for the use of leisure time.

Men must be prepared to meet necessary demands for a life of a certain kind. If the preparations take up much time and energy one might arrive at the paradoxical result that a man might use up all his spare time getting himself ready for leisure. We can escape from this difficulty by having a good deal of the educating and training for leisure carried out early in life. Today we tend to be satisfied instead to fill spare time with activities that require little or no preparation. In that way we make possible a longer period of spare time. But the length of a stretch does not matter if it contains nothing but zeros.

The problem of leisure time will not be solved if the problem is not recognized to be germinally present in childhood. Then, and at later stages, each person should be completed in such a way that he will be prompted to move on until he finally arrives at the point when he can fulfill his promise to be a civilized man. Gradually brought to be a part of civilized mankind, with its multiple treasures, he will learn to turn his spare time into a leisure time where he enjoys the goods of mankind and perhaps helps increase its store.

There must be some who see to it that the amount of spare time available to others is maximized by altering the conditions of work, thereby cutting down the amount of time and energy there consumed. There must also be those who see to it that the spare time so provided is used most advantageously. Some men must work at the problem of providing opportunities for a proper use of spare time, if the spare time of the rest of men is to be a time of true leisure. The work of both groups involves a concern for conditions and facilities, and a knowledge of what men want and ought to want, what they can do, and what they can be taught to do. No one can claim to have all the relevant knowledge. More, those who are primarily involved in the work of making whatever is known in this area have practical importance usually have not time enough to learn just what the ultimate outcome of a leisured life is or ought to be. But some knowledge of what man is and ought to be can be achieved by men who, in their leisure time, reflect and speculate.

4]

The time that is spent on harmless pleasures—
card games, spectator sports, amateur theatricals,
light reading—may enable a man to work better after-
wards. Considered apart from that fact, these activities
merely fill up idle time. They are desirable only because
they make that idle time a time that is pleasant. They then
help one not only to avoid boredom but to have some simple
joys. Such joys are good in themselves; often they yield desirable self-knowledge and insight; one's grasp of oneself
and others is sometimes deepened by them. But an idle
time, even one filled with joys, is but a series of easy mo-
ments set over against the rest of the day. It is to be sharply
distinguished from leisure time, which is never occupied
with trivialities, and may have many periods of tension,
frustration, and even of sacrifice and self-denial.

Leisure time has no "use" if by "use" one intends to
refer to what is only a means to some external end. But it
can and does have a use in two other senses. What is done
in leisure time may be economically valuable, even though
what is done then is not done so as to produce that outcome. Research, artistic activity, and reflection yield results that are marketable—usually when they pay no attention to the market. In leisure time too a good life is not only
promoted but is exactly what is then realized. Leisure time
is a time best used by a civilized man.

A good life is no mosaic of alternating periods of
leisure and work. It is a life in which leisure gives meaning
and direction to whatever other time one has. Leisure,
unlike recreational time, though it does not make more
efficient work possible, except incidentally, does make it
more meaningful. What is achieved in that time makes
worktime a period when basic values are exhibited, even

though what one is engaged in doing is itself not of much importance. The writing of advertisements, the driving of a truck, the manufacture of shoes gain in significance when brought within the orbit of values and appreciations which are germane to whatever else a man does.

In leisure time one engages in activities that are good in themselves and good for what is good in itself. To discover what these activities are, we must begin by taking account of man's potentialities and noting what must be done to best fulfill them. The best activities are those which are internally variable and have an extended field of operation, for these allow a man's potentialities to be realized again and again. How many of these are there? Surely, as many as there are types of channels through which a man can make himself manifest, and obtain what he needs. Even a short list of them will have to include health, knowledge, self-expression, character formation, personality, and self-adjustment, for each of these is a good in itself and makes possible its own continuance.

Being healthy is a good in itself; it gives tonality to the entire life and all one does. When we are in good health we act without impediment in the use of our energies and in the selection of our goals. If not merely lived through but carried out in engagements in sports and exercise, our health makes its own continuance and sometimes even its own increase possible.

Knowledge is itself a good. He who knows has laid hold of what is not himself and thereby has added other realities to his own to become more perfect, more complete. When the knowledge is merely factual, a tissue of items of information, it is merely good in itself. When it is guided and controlled by principles of inquiry, a lively curiosity, and general ideas, it becomes a stronger form of knowledge, grounding the possibility of further knowledge. To help men share in this kind of knowledge in their leisure time, use should be made of libraries, museums, and adult educational programs. These agencies function best if interest and taste have been cultivated quite early; otherwise more likely than not men will use them mainly to fill up idle time.

The arts are now widely known to offer final goods to be enjoyed and lived with. They do not lose this value if they are also actively engaged in. The activity not only makes possible a greater sensitivity, but provides one with an insight into the nature of creativity and the reality that only the arts directly reveal.

No one knows what creative powers he has until he has experimented with multiple media, techniques, and instruments. Such experimentation should begin quite early, when the body is flexible, the mind open, and wonder easily awakened. Continued into whatever spare time is available, an active interest in the arts will yield a leisure time that can enrich the rest of the day.

Virtue is a habit achieved through the repetition of acts of virtue. Many virtues intertwined constitute a good character. This is a good in itself. It could be made to ground the achievement of still other virtues, a firmer character. This is done in leisure time by giving men the opportunity to test themselves in adventures with nature, with one another, and within themselves. Hikes, climbs, contests, explorations, endurance trials, and the like are ways of achieving the double end of having and producing character in leisure time.

The personality is the person made evident. It is not a matter of agreeableness or charm, but rather of a self-acceptance with an acceptance of others as of equal significance. It is to be oneself in oneself together with others who are then and there helped to be themselves. The result is excellent men, severally and together. Celebrations, rituals, communal activities, and above all the living in the light of what one takes to be a final assessment by God, not only sustain and strengthen the personality but guide one toward its further enrichment.

Religion is a leisure-time activity. We turn it into work

when we engage in magic, or when we convert prayers into petitions. Religion involves one with God and thereby provides a new value for the rest of one's activities. It is also an avenue through which one finds oneself and learns how to adjust to oneself and to others.

The finding of oneself and the adjustment of oneself to others is also promoted by engaging in common enterprises which make for the concretionalization of the prevailing myths and ideologies. When men sing and dance together, when they tell stories and exercise their imaginations, they provide frames in which each can find a place. When the self-adjustment serves as a spur to a deeper and firmer mastery of oneself by oneself and in relation to others, the self-adjustment becomes a good in itself which casts a radiance over whatever is done in work or play.

In each one of these ways leisure time becomes a time when men are at their best. The excellence of the activities engaged in during leisure makes it desirable to continue them at other times. It is for this reason that some men reverse the usual attitudes toward work and leisure, and try to work mainly at that which is a continuation of what they do when they have leisure. When they return to work, the level of maturity and control that they managed to reach in leisure defines the nature and affects the tone of what they then do. Though these results are not the object of leisure, they are the inevitable products of a well-spent leisure time. The fortunate worker is a complete man who became complete in his leisure time.

Athletes, scientists, philosophers, artists, the religious, and ethical leaders live unitary lives in which the excellence obtainable during leisure ennobles whatever other work they might engage in. In their work they tend to realize the same ends that concern them during leisure. Even when they are forced to attend to the demands of brute existence, they do so in a spirit which leisure time alone made it possible for them to acquire. If they teach or assume some public position they express the very values they had already embodied. These men offer models of what all men are to do with their lives. In their different ways they tell them to find that kind of work which continues the desirable activities of a correctly used leisure time, and to make everything else that is done act as carriers of the great values that had been achieved.

Leisure is the time when men are most mature, the time when it is possible for them to make the rest of their day as excellent as possible, giving it a new value and perhaps a new objective. The good life is a life in which a rich leisure gives direction and meaning to all else that is done.

Since men must somehow live together, and since they all belong to an eventual civilization embracing all mankind, they should also in leisure learn how to sustain and supplement one another. This is a difficult problem. I think we ought at last to attend to it, for its solution summarizes and adds meaning to much of the foregoing.

7

The Good Life

BY ACCEPTING HIS PAST, the mature man becomes a vital part of a civilized present, where he contributes to the world about to be. That contribution need not be major. It may not even be the outcome of an attempt to produce anything new or of consequence. It may follow on purely supportive acts, on honest ongoing appreciations, or on an enjoyment of a common inheritance. The support and vitalization make contributions, not to the content, but to the being, and to the continuance and appeal of a civilized life. A man can be part of and contribute to that life even if he is only a learner and not a teacher, a disciple and not a master, if he preserves and does not innovate. And he contributes most, not by thinking of making contributions, but by involving himself in tasks and problems which are geared to outside realities.

Civilization is an outcome, not a goal. It is the result of man's concern with things sometimes much smaller than civilization, such as his own or his nation's well-being, and with things sometimes much grander, such as the stars, the cosmos, or God. It would be good for knowledge and for civilization if men were to attend to all of these in all possible ways. But no one has the time or the ability to engage in such a stupendous task. Still, though no one can engage himself with signal success in activities which relate to all of these, it is rarely that anyone becomes so involved with one that he loses all relation to the rest.

We have two main choices: to try to partake of all that is good, but at the price of not being able to master anything, or to be in full possession of a limited number of excellences while benefiting from the presence of what other men produce. If we are not to be dilettantes or poetasters we cannot do better than to take the second of these alternatives. And this means, I think, that each of us must engage in only some of a number of the basic enterprises that are devoted to the attainment of civilized goods.

2]

There is more than one basic enterprise. Some are concerned with acquiring, conserving, or transmitting knowledge; some deal with the production and use of material goods; others are occupied with the creation and enjoyment of the arts, or with the pursuit of and participation in ethical or religious values. No one of these objectives can be replaced by others, but each is so broad and basic that it provides a place for the products of the others, though of course only in its own terms.

Whatever one enterprise includes within its own confines it subjects to its own categories, meanings, and values. It allows for the enjoyment of all the others, but only in subordinate roles, with their meanings and values set in an alien field. Evidently, we cannot be content with having only one perspective on whatever there is, but must instead learn how to profit from all as on a footing and thus as equally basic and effective. To achieve this result three things must be done.

There must be 1) a complete giving of oneself to some one enterprise; 2) a detachment from the fruits of it while they are made available to all and 3) a coordination of all enterprises as well as of the goods they produce. The result will be the creation of a shared treasury of excellence. He who is at the center of such a treasury lives the richest possible human life if he adds to his own spirit the attitudes which others sustain in their pursuit of their distinctive goals.

1) Each man looks at the world in terms of a set of values gradually accreted over the years, partly through the help of others. Gradually he builds up a perspective on all that exists and is known, though it is doubtful that any man stays completely with it. The most inclusive perspectives are the *humanistic*, which concentrates on the values that make for human welfare, growth, and freedom; the *idealistic* which attends to the basic prescriptions, goals, possibilities, and myths that govern society; the *naturalistic*, which sees man and other realities in this space-time world as part of a single whole, governed by its own intrinsic laws; and the *religious* which evaluates man and the rest of the universe in terms of their capacity to enrich one another in a single, final harmony. Each demands the full measure of a man's loyalty. Each is worthy of taking up all of his time, energy, and concentration. But justice to any one will inevitably require a neglect of the others. A commitment to one set of values precludes a proper pursuit of the others.

It is only when a man specializes in some one basic enterprise that it is possible for him to realize properly one set of values. If he is properly educated though he will know and be ready to affirm that other sets of values are as basic, and are pursued with as much sincerity and with the same desirable outcome as is his own.

A good school puts a young man on the road to being civilized by critically introducing him to the basic fields of human endeavor. It introduces him to the major enterprises, and enables him to savor the primary values and achievements of civilization. The broader the scope of his education, the more does it grant his diverse powers independent but supplementing roles. By making his self, character, person, and knowledge interplay, the school helps him to become more at home with himself, fellowman, society, world, and cosmos. Unfortunately, only a few ever fully give themselves to any enterprise. There is perhaps none who, while devoted to the pursuit of one or two enterprises, is incidentally involved with and appreciative of the full importance of all the others. But this only indicates that there is an objective still to be attained.

2) A man can be said to be properly involved in a basic enterprise if he contributes its results to a common treasury. If he does this he will, while actively involved with only some goods, be able to benefit from the fact that others are equally involved elsewhere. From this position the civilized world appears to be a collection of goods produced and shared in by individual, dedicated men. Each man there has a steady core in the shape of a persistent character and a disciplined outlook, where diverse faculties are expressed in harmony, and the values that he individually pursues are interlocked with those of importance to others. He is a central man, environed as he is by the totality of man's achievements in a single commonwealth which he sustains, and to which he contributes.

A central man has a firm core. Gradually he has managed to satisfy the different facets of his nature. While environed by the world he is detached from it; knowing how to use his powers in harmony, he appreciates the necessity for a plurality of enterprises all encompassing whatever there is. Initially and throughout he maintains his sense of wonder, and exhibits a genuine interest in and concern for the complexity and dignity of whatever there is. Giving each thing and enterprise its due in attention and consideration, he is the embodiment of the virtue of justice.

There may never have been and there may never be such a paragon. But the prospect should define our tasks and obligations. Such an ideal gives education its aim and therefore shows it in what direction it is to move.

Formal education enables a man to make a lifelong effort to be one of a plurality of focal points in a world of civilized goods. The fact that few or none may ever be perfectly educated does not make undesirable the effort to come as close to that result as one can. But no one can hope to approximate it who has not in childhood managed to achieve a cherished self, who has not in youth become self-disciplined and organized, and who has not as a young man become acquainted with many enterprises.

3) We cannot rest with this conclusion since it forces us to suppose that the most civilized of men will be an active specialist in one area, but will share only incidentally or superficially in the rest. We can move on though if we attend to the fact that each enterprise not only subordinates the others (as was previously remarked) but rightly does so. Different enterprises are to be seen to function alongside one another at the same time that they are acknowledged to operate within the limits that the others provide. He who is occupied with knowledge is not engaged in producing a work of art, but he can deal with art, though to be sure only in intellectual terms, and even take it to be a special way of cognizing. At the same time he can recognize that knowledge, from the perspective of art, is a kind of creative act and even a special type of fine art which reveals rather than communicates, enriches rather than informs. He who was primarily occupied with knowledge will then not only pursue it as a finality but at the same time appreciate it as having another value and meaning from another perspective. He will as a consequence find himself, his enterprise and its goods, in every area of civilization, in one of which they will be primary and in the others of which they will be subordinate.

No one can know what a basic enterprise is like who does not see that it must both subordinate all the others and be alongside them. Yet, since no one can actually engage in every basic enterprise, no one can actually experience the others as subordinating the rest. A man who subordinates others to his own basic enterprise will not experience it as that which is in fact subordinated by those others. This though need not prevent him from sharing in the attitude of the men who give themselves to other enterprises. While his enterprise subordinates the others, and while he is aware but does not experience the fact that they subordinate his, he can accept as part of his own attitude, the attitudes that govern them.

A student of knowledge is critical, analytical, and speculative. If he is appreciative of the attitude that governs the artist he will introduce into the process of knowledge something of the artist's adventuresomeness, spontaneity, freedom, and creativity. He will also share with those who are involved in service the need to be efficient, well-organized, and effective, exercising prudence and foresight. And, with religious men, he will combine humility with generosity, backed by a confidence in the eventual conquest of the good.

Each of these three ways of dealing with perspectives has serious limitations, mainly because they have been dealt with in isolation from one another. Combined, their limitations are overcome. The mature civilized man is then seen to be one who, pursuing his own enterprise as basic (and thus as subordinating the others while he learns to accept the texture which his enterprise acquires by being subordinate to the others), adopts as his own the spirit that animates the others, at the same time that he contributes to and shares in a common treasury of goods. If he be religious he will take religion to subordinate philosophy, science, art, family, state, and history, but will remain aware of the way religion is grasped from their positions. And he will enrich his piety, charity, and submission by adopting the clarity and precision of the student of knowledge, the structure and stability of the institutional man, and the freedom and control of the creative man. Only then will he be a full part of a single civilization to which he contributes and of which he partakes.

This formulation of the nature of the truly civilized is highly general, and tends to blur the truth that all the basic enterprises are internally complex. All in fact have a number of subdivisions, each of which claims to be inclusive of the other subdivisions. Knowledge may be directed toward what is daily confronted, leading to the formulation of scientific hypotheses dealing with the whole of space and time; toward the nature of what is possible and necessary, leading to the study of mathematics; toward what is demanded of man by whatever is final and permanent, leading to an interest in religion and theology; or toward knowing what is ultimately real, the topic of philosophy. He whose major concern is with science will look at philosophy and its results in terms of scientific categories, or as sources of suggestions and vague surmises to be scientifically sharpened and pursued. He will not be sufficiently appreciative though of the nature of philosophy unless he knows that from the perspective of philosophy science has a position alongside other forms of knowledge, where its claims, procedures, and status are philosophically evaluated. His scientific temper should be infected with the radical sympathy and self-criticism characteristic of the true philosopher. He and the philosopher will then not only contribute to a common world of knowledge and share in it, but they will do so as men who are masters of specialized ways of knowing, and yet appreciative of the rights of the other ways of knowing and the spirit that animates them.

3]

Nothing has as yet been said of what men together might produce and be. Our account will be incomplete so long as it fails to find room for the group achievements of business, politics, engineering, transportation, communication, and merchandising. Treated as occupied solely with means for the production of further means they serve merely to make a civilized world possible. But they have a more important role. They all contribute to civilization when pursued as group activities involved with means for a final end.

He who is interested solely in making a profit is occupied with only a means to a means. But a man can be directly productive of what could satisfy basic human needs, with profit occurring as an incidental concomitant. He will then work at a means for an end. Were a politician to take his major task to be the production of peace and prosperity rather than the increase of his power, he could achieve a similar civilized status. So could an engineer who was primarily concerned with controlling, subduing, and using natural forces so as to adjust men to the world about. Through their organizations, machinery, and work, such men radically affect the nature of civilization. If they work cooperatively for the sake of a final end, they are part of civilization.

If civilization is pictured as a set of concentric circles, these men will form its outer ring. Sharing in the concern for excellence characteristic of those closest to the center, they will help make possible its presence and preservation.

This way of putting the matter takes the position of those near the center. The positions can be reversed. Assuming the position of those who are at the outer ring, we can see them as they see themselves—loyal members of various groups or wholes. Those at the center now appear to be detached individuals, only minimally involved in the desirable cooperative activity of making men as secure and prosperous as they have a right to be.

The perspective of those at the inner and those on the outer ring are not on a footing. It is better to be near the center than at a distance from it. But it would be better still to share in the values and gain from the wholes produced by those on the outer ring. This can be done in four ways: First, the wholes have a qualitative nature; a plurality of them provides a variety of tonalities. By allowing these tonalities to affect it the inner ring acquires a variety of accents and thereby avoids becoming monotonous and aggregational. Second, different wholes sustain different intensive relations among men and goods, thereby providing them with new roles. Each man because of his place within a whole is enhanced in status and can with the others help the rest in ways he alone cannot. Members of wholes by working with others contribute to the satisfaction of the needs of the individuals near the center. Third, the achievements of a whole can be distributively credited to those near the center. They thereby acquire the status of vicarious producers and possessors of what had been obtained elsewhere. Fourth, those near the center can be brought into relation with one another by means of the relation which the various wholes have to one another. Interrelated by means of the wholes that productive men provide, those near the center will then act as representatives of one another, acquiring a meaning from the intimate way they are interrelated and the way they function. As a consequence, the relations between them will have a complexity and power they could not have had before.

Dr. Marcia Guttentag has made me aware of a dynamic element which should be introduced into this account. Men pursuing one type of life should also bear testimony to the need to support what is excellent in other types. He who was primarily concerned with inquiry or art should think of himself as part of a steady stream of men which may, through marches, demonstrations, and public declarations, for example, testify against some political injustice. He who gave himself to a life on the outer ring should similarly think of himself as one who will, through financial aid and by opposition to political control, censorship and the like, testify to the importance of what is done in the inner ring. In both cases, without losing their dedication to a particular type of life, the men will then not only benefit from what is gained in other pursuits, but will effectively support the types of life there followed.

The complete man is never merely a detached unit member of civilization with its common treasury of goods. In attitude and act, he exhibits the meanings and values that accrue to those who work cooperatively with others, thereby acquiring a representative character and power. But then ought not the educational process have included within it a program directed toward teaching men to become vital parts of groups, to be productive, to be cooperative members of societies, nations, and states? Is not traditional educational theory on the right track in its insistence that the student be taught to become a productive adult and a good citizen? I think not, for two reasons: this aspect has already been taken care of in the schools, and it ought not to be attended to there.

The cooperation and the loyalties adults exhibit are the very virtues that the student learned in school, particularly in the gymnasium and on the playing field. Though he was not taught the particular techniques appropriate to this or that type of organization, he was trained to be a good member of whatever organization he was a part. Throughout his school career the student has already learned the lesson which society and business carry on.

Yet we ought not to focus on that training. It is desirable only if it is a consequence of an educational system which aims at nothing other than the making of civilized men through the teaching of useless subjects. All of us are too quickly and surely caught within economic and political nets; we are all so subject to the pressures of society, state, and need, that it is unnecessary—even undesirable—for an educational effort to have us look in the direction of practice.

Commerce and society operate steadily and powerfully to turn men into merely public beings. At their best, and without a counterpoise, they would produce men who were good together but not good severally. Because the public world will have most men firmly in its grip, it is necessary to teach them how to find a place and time for another side of themselves. Practical life must be matched by an equally powerful force of a civilizing education. We must balance its otherwise successful influence by teaching men to be detached from the world so that they can make themselves into private beings concerned with eternal truths and values.

All organizations are the family writ large. Born into the family, with attachments we never wholly break, we are by habit, want, and obstacle made to be part of other groups. Our hopes may be directed elsewhere; we may spend most of our thought and effort on other matters. But we will always be informally habituated and have some attachment to others. Our informal learning should be supplemented by a formal instruction. Then practically grounded and justified wholes will become occasions for our leisurely discovery of the meaning of order, law, loyalty, and cooperation.

It is education that enables men to be civilized, while necessity and experience interrelate them in various effective groups. They become complete men when, while remaining parts of such groups, they function as full, individual members of a common civilization; or alternatively, when, while individually sharing in a common treasury of civilized goods, they cooperate with others to make valuable combinations of themselves and of those goods. From the position of this ideal the almost senseless bustle of history takes on the semblance of order, the labor of generations acquires lasting significance, the forced choices of men have the power of free decisions, and the limited things men do assume the form of universality.

Men must re-create themselves to be themselves fulfilled. They are made in many ways, but the best has always proved to be a making of themselves, under the guidance of those who have already gone part of the distance and who make evident to the rest how good it would be to move at least that far as well. All, to make themselves excellently, must learn the art of combination. They must unite what had been taught in the process of becoming civilized with what they have learned in the course of working with one another.

The best of men is a public being who lives a private life alongside others. Near the center of a civilized world, he is also somehow at its periphery, directly or indirectly involved in the making and use of means. His work makes leisure possible, and his leisure makes his work worthwhile. A wise man, his knowledge sustains and is sustained by practice.

Index

Adolescence: age span of, 38
Adult: as practical man, 65
Analysis, 82
Anthropology: and realities, 89; and society, 90; and religion, 91; and limited settings, 98
Arithmetic and child, 23–25
Art(s): education as an, 17; and tween-age, 49; in youth's curriculum, 61; of living, and college, 65; and college curriculum, 85–88; history of, 85; making of, 85; teaching of, 87, 95; essence of, 88; philosopher of, 88; and realities, 89; actively engaged in, 138; and enterprises, 145
Artists as teachers, 85
Attitudes and education, 65

Background: freeing oneself from one's, 37
Behaviorists, 89–90
Biology: teaching of, 58; taught to youth, 96
Body: youth's explorations of, 48

Catering to child, 20
Central man, 144
Character: building, and education, 46; good, and virtue, 138

Chemistry: teaching of, 57–58; as college course, 71–72
Child: as a child, 3, 6; teaching of, 3, 16; past of, 4; properly loved, 5; and mother's love, 6; teacher's love for, 6; teacher's sympathy for, 7; allowing a present to, 8; living in world of his own, 8–9; rapid maturation, 8; play of, 9–11; and sports, 10; imagination of, 11; play as education, 11; rights of, and courts, 11; toys of, 11; learning of, 12; stories for, 12–16, 42; and existence, 13; and exactitude, 18; and reading, 20–22; catering to, 20; and speech, 22–23; and arithmetic, 23–25; and social code, 25; and tests, 26; well-taught, 27; quality of acts of, 39; and responsibility, 40–41; and sympathy, 40, 42; and temperance, 42; and maximum freedom, 43; and leisure time, 135
Civilization: as totality of values, 75; and labor, 111; as outcome, 141
Coaches and youth, 48–49
College: attendance at, 47–48; as preparatory for professional schools, 63; desired product of, 64; and art of living, 65; as research

institution, 69; teaching in, 69; and unity, 70; teachers, 71; comprehensive courses in, 73; curriculum, 67, 77–110; philosopher's role in, 83
Communism, 93–94
Confidence and youth, 40
Cooperation, 150
Courage and youth, 42
Courts and rights of child, 11
Craft and tween-age, 49
Craftsmanship, 112
Creativity and education, 66
Criticism: and youth, 44; in philosophy, 82
Culture: freeing oneself from, 37
Curriculum: of secondary schools, 47, 54; college, 67, 77–110

Demands of men, 126
Democracy, 93–94
Dentistry, 72–73

Economics, 101
Education: child's play as, 11; as an art, 17; satisfying and dissatisfying the student, 31; beginning in wonder, 33; task of, 34; and character building, 46; of young men, 63; and attitudes, 65; and creativity, 66; continuing late into life, 107; and finalities, 113; and full life, 118; and fulfillment, 127
Emotions and youth, 49–50
Engineering, 101–2
Enterprise: basic, 142–45
Exactitude and child, 18
Exercise, 103
Existence and child, 13
Experimentation and science, 98

Fame, 124–25
Family, 151
Finalities and education, 113
Freedom for the child, 43
Fulfillment: of student, 38; and education, 127

Games and child, 10

God, 92, 138
Good: health as a, 137; knowledge as a, 137; the good life, 141–52
Good Child, The (sonnet), 9
Government: courses in, 93; and economic affairs, 113; and the good life, 114
Graduate schools, 105–6
Guidance of youth, 44
Guttentag, Marcia, 149

Happiness, 47
Health: as a good, 137
History: in secondary school, 58–59; of philosophy, 80; of art, 85; different types of, 87–88
Humanistic values, 143

Idealistic values, 143
Idle time, 128
Imagination of child, 11
Infant: needs of, 5–6
Inquiry: controlled, 97

Judgments and fame, 125

Kittens: play of, 10
Knowing, 121
Knowledge: and training, 95; as a good, 137; and art, 145; student of, 146

Labor and civilization, 111
Language and the child, 22–23
Laws of behavior, 89
Leaders: public, 117; religious, 117
Learning: of child, 12; rote-learning, 19; struggle involved in, 121
Leisure time: and school, 132; and work, 132; program for, 133; and child, 135; and religion, 138–39
Life(ves): of child, 3–30; full, of educated man, 37; the good, 38, 141–52; lives men lead, 111–26; and service, 114–15; the good, and government, 114; and use of mind, 116

Living: as ripening, 8; art of, and college, 65
Logic: as college course, 77, 80–81; modern, 80–81
Love: parental, 5; properly loved child, 5; limits of mother's, 6; teacher's for child, 6; as opening oneself up, 7
Loyalty, 150

Man(men): educated, full life of, 37; young, age span of, 39; young, education of, 63; practical, adult as, 65; lives men lead, 111–26; mature, 116; secure, 125; demands of, 126; fulfilled, 127; needs of, 130; acceptance of past, 141; central, 144; involved in basic enterprise, 144; mature civilized, 146; truly civilized, 147; being together, 148–52; producing together, 148–52; complete, 150; recreating himself, 151
Manhood: on the verge of, 63–76
Mathematicians: using their minds, 84
Mathematics: teaching of, 33, 36, 55–56; and college curriculum, 77, 83–85; and possibility, 84; and truth, 84; science and mathematical form, 98
Maturation of child, 8
Maturity, 118
Mind(s): of tween-agers, 52–53; of mathematicians, 84; use of, and better life, 116
Mother: love for child, 6
Music, 86

Naturalistic values, 143
Needs of man, 130

Observation and youth, 58

Painting, 86
Parents: guidance of children, 4; parental love, 5
Past: of child, 4; acceptance of, by man, 141

Peace, 113
Personality, 138
Philosopher: becoming a, 79; role in college, 83; of art, 88
Philosophic inquiry, 78
Philosophy: as adventure, 77; in college curriculum, 77; reasons for being taught to the young, 79; history of, 80; questions asked by, 80; of sport, 104
Physics: teaching of, 57; and sociology, 77; in college curriculum, 99–100
Play of child, 9–11
Pleasure: good and bad, 120–21; and power, 123–24
Poetry: teaching of, 33
Political science, 93
Politics: in secondary school, 58–59; realities of, 60; and realities, 89; teaching of, 94; problems of, 113
Possibility and mathematics, 84
Poverty, 114
Power: and pleasure, 123–24; and wealth, 123; misuse of, 124
Prediction and science, 99
Present: allowing a present to a child, 8
Principles, 77
Production, 111–12, 115
Professional schools, 105–6
Psychiatrists, 117–18
Psychology: in college curriculum, 89–90, 98; and religion, 91
Public leaders, 117
Puppies: play of, 10

Rationality of youth, 53
Reading: and child, 20–22; fast and slow, discussion of, 21; good, 21–22
Reality(ies): that transcend the world, 75; that ground all else, 77; ultimate, 81; and art, 89
Reasonableness of youth, 53
Reasoning and youth, 55

Rebellion and tween-agers, 41
Recreational time, 128, 131
Religion: and youth, 51–52; as social science, 89, 91–92; teaching of, 92; and leisure time, 138–39
Religious leaders, 117
Religious values, 143
Research institution: college as a, 69
Responsibility: and child, 40–41; and youth, 41
Rote-learning, 19

Status, 124
School(s): elementary, 18–19; task of, 34; secondary, 47, 48; secondary, curriculum of, 54: graduate, 105–6; professional, 105–6; and leisure, 132
Science: teaching of, 33, 56–57, 95–96; social, 89; political, 93; as controlled inquiry, 97; and experimentation, 98; and mathematical form, 98; and prediction, 99
Sculpture, 86
Security, 125–26
Self-acceptance, 138
Service: life of, 114–15
Siblings, 4
Social code and child, 25
Social science, 89
Societal patterns and youth, 41
Sociology: and physics, 72; in college curriculum, 89, 90, 97; and religion, 91
Spare time: definition of, 128; uses of, 129–31; as burden, 133
Speculation, 82
Speech and child, 22–23
Sport(s): and child, 10; in college curriculum, 102–4; philosophy of, 104
Stories for child, 12–16, 42
Student(s): as teacher, 36; fulfillment of, 38; learning from one another, 105; of knowledge, 146
Survey courses in college, 73

Sympathy and the child, 7, 40, 43

Teacher: love for child, 6; sympathy for child, 7; as sympathetic older companion, 12; good, 35; reasons for becoming a, 35–36; as student, 36; college, 61; artist as, 85
Teaching: of child, 3; formal, of child, 16; of mathematics, 33, 36, 55–56; of poetry, 33; of science, 33, 56, 95–96; object of, 37; of chemistry, 57–58; of physics, 57; of biology, 58; of history, 59; in colleges, loss of interest in, 69; of arts, 87, 95; of religion, 92; of politics, 94
Teen-age, the, 38
Temperance and the child, 42
Tests and the child, 26
Time: and the biologist, 100. See also Idle time; Leisure time; Recreational time; Spare time
Toys of child, 11
Tradition, 37–38
Training and knowledge, 95
Truth and mathematics, 84
Tween-age: definition of, 39; and rebellion, 41; and art, 49; and craft, 49. See also Youth
Tween-ager: mind of, 52–53

Unity and college, 70
Universities: composition of, 106–7; American, 106; Continental, 106; English, 106

Values: civilization as totality of, 75; and fame, 125; humanistic, 143; idealistic, 143; naturalistic, 143; religious, 143
Virtue, 138

Wars: and youth, 51; peace as interlude between, 113–14

Wealth: and power, 122–23; as means, 122; accumulation of, 123

Wisdom, 132

Wonder: education beginning in, 33

Work: and child, 10; and pride, 112; and leisure, 132

Workmanship, 112

World and ultimate realities, 75

Youth: age span of, 38; quality of acts of, 39; confidence of, 40; and responsibility, 41; and societal patterns, 41; and courage, 42; and criticism, 44; and guidance, 44; in world of his own, 44; protection of himself, 44; helped to find himself, 45; and coaches, 48–49; explorations of body, 48; and emotions, 49–50; and religion, 51–52; and wars, 51; rationality of, 53; reasonableness of, 53; and reasoning, 55; and observation, 58; and realities of politics, 60; and art, 61; properly educated, qualities of, 63–64; and philosophy, 79. *See also* Tween-age